Deep Down
Character Change through the Fruit of the Spirit

Tim Riter

DEEP

CHARACTER CHANGE THROUGH THE FRUIT OF THE SPIRIT

DOWN

Tyndale House Publishers, Inc.
Wheaton, Illinois

Library of Congress Cataloging-in-Publication Data

Riter, Tim, date
    Deep down : character change through the Fruit of the Spirit / Tim Riter.
      p.   cm.
    ISBN 0-8423-1797-X (sc)
    1. Christian life.   2. Fruit of the Spirit.   3. Character.
  I. Title.
    BV4501.2.R573   1995   95-13606

Printed in the United States of America

01   00   99   98   97   96   95
7   6   5   4   3   2   1

Deep Down is dedicated to the most awesome friend this man
has — a friend who stands for righteousness,
and forgives with grace:
my Lord, Jesus Christ.

And to a very special friend, who has stuck with me through it
all — a friend who also stands for righteousness,
and forgives with grace:
my wife, Sheila.

CONTENTS

Acknowledgments ix

PART 1: DEEP-DOWN CHARACTER CHANGE

1 *Character Change: A Vital Need?* 3
2 *A Roadmap for Change* 17

PART 2: NINE CHRISTIAN CHARACTER TRAITS

3 *Getting beyond Ourselves: Love* 33
4 *Smiling through the Tears: Joy* 51
5 *Slowing Our Spirit: Peace* 69
6 *Hanging in There: Patience* 81
7 *Kind to the Bone: Kindness* 93
8 *Moral Fiber: Goodness* 105
9 *Keeping Commitments: Faithfulness* 121
10 *Choosing Our Response: Gentleness* 137
11 *Doing What We Most Desire: Self-Control* 151

PART 3: MAKING CHARACTER CHANGES

12 *Grabbing God's Gusto: Being Filled with the Spirit* . . 167

ACKNOWLEDGMENTS

My thanks to

Lamont Lee, for insights into distinctions between character, personality, and behavior;

Lynn Vanderzalm, for guiding this rookie author through the wilds of refining his thoughts;

Ken Petersen and the Tyndale family, for believing a rookie's concepts were worth taking the risk;

Jerry Christensen, for his help in crafting the questions.

ONE

Deep-Down
Character Change

CHAPTER 1

Character Change: A Vital Need?

Gary, would you stick around a minute?" Hal asked quietly as the real-estate agents drifted homeward out of the office. Gary knew instantly that his broker didn't want to talk business. All day Hal had seemed distracted, his normally quick business mind running in slow motion. And the deep lines on his face spelled trouble and inner pain.

The words caught in Hal's throat. "It's my son, Mike. He's really in trouble. . . . I'm not much of a churchgoer, but since you've been going to church, I've seen you change quite a bit. I know you and Mike used to be close. Maybe some God-talk could straighten him out."

"I would be glad to talk to Mike," Gary answered. "What's the problem?"

"He's on drugs," Hal said, eyes downcast. "Some of the people at his new job were at a bar, and a fight broke out. The cops came and found some cocaine on him. They took him to jail. I'm so mad at him that I don't know if I want to bail him out or not. Besides, I think he may be cheating on Susie, his wife." Hal's normally gruff veneer cracked along with his voice. "He talks a lot about this woman at work, and it makes me uneasy. I don't know what I would do if he really is cheating because my grandsons are so special. They don't need a druggie for a dad—even if he is my son."

Later that night, as Gary drove to the jail, he wondered how open Mike would be. Lately, Mike had seemed uncomfortable around him. Now Gary realized Mike's guilty conscience must have been bothering him. Perhaps jail would be a reality check, where Mike would be brought face-to-face with the consequences of his choices.

Mike smiled broadly when he saw Gary in the meeting room. And he listened when Gary shared with grace, compassion, and firmness what God can do in a life. After he got out of jail, Mike began attending church and a Bible study and soon accepted Christ. Not long afterward, Susie also accepted Christ. Aware of her own need for God, she had already started going to church. She was amazed at Mike's quick grasp of Christianity and his hunger for the Bible.

But slowly, the spiritual euphoria wore off. The initial burst of Bible study and church gave way to going when it was convenient, and convenient seldom arrived. When he started using drugs again, Susan found out and threatened to leave him. He was frantic, so he showed up again at church.

Although Mike made it through the crisis, a pattern developed. And over the next several years, the church cycled through that pattern several times with him. At each new predicament he would come back to church, crying, distraught, begging for advice. But that advice was seldom followed. When the woman at work got involved, Susie finally had enough. She filed for divorce. Now, years later, Mike and Susie have only minimal contact. He sees his three children only occasionally and sends child-support checks even more sporadically. Mike and Susie's dreams of a lifetime together vanished into the wind.

What was Mike's problem? He knew what a relationship with God was all about. He obeyed God, for a short time, on minor issues. He had faith, at least on the surface. But it never stuck. He never seemed to let God get deep enough inside him for any change to take place.

IS CHANGE REQUIRED IN CHRISTIANITY?

Some Christian teachers say that no changes are required when a person accepts Christ, just a simple affirmation of belief—no repentance, no transformation. The popularity of this position is astounding yet understandable. We've all heard people say, "That's just the way I am. You have to accept me." That attitude reveals a fundamental misunderstanding that Christianity is a change of who we are.

A study done by the Roper Organization in 1990 explored the behavior of "born-again Christians" before and after conversion. The results were shocking. Of the 1,975 people surveyed, 27 percent said they consider themselves born again. Behavior in three major areas was evaluated: the use of illegal drugs, driving while intoxicated, and marital infidelity. Without exception, behavior after conversion grew worse in each category. For instance, 2 percent acknowledged marital infidelity before conversion, and 5 percent after conversion. Numerous other studies show similar results.

Why are so many Christians like non-Christians? What happened to the challenge Paul made in Romans 12:2, that we should be transformed? What happened to Jesus' clear statement in John 14:15, that if we love him, we will obey what he commanded? These questions are ones we will address throughout this book.

Not all believers have missed the behavior change God

intends at conversion. The marvelous 1905 revival in Wales is one glowing example. One hundred thousand baptisms occurred in six months, and Wales became a different place. Overall arrests decreased 40 percent. In 1902, 11,282 arrests were made for drunkenness; in 1905, fewer than five thousand arrests were made. A single story from that period exemplifies the life change going on in Wales: A local magistrate usually heard cases Friday evening, all day Saturday, and half of Sunday. After the revival, the bailiff appeared before the judge one weekend wearing white gloves, signifying no cases were to be heard. The Welsh Christians had experienced deep-down changes that rocked their society.

Why don't all Christians experience these changes? For many people, the answer isn't theological. They believe repentance plays a vital role in faith and that obedience is an integral part. They're not intentionally trying to avoid living the Christian life. But I think Mark Twain expressed the problem succinctly when he quipped, "It's not the things in the Bible I don't understand that bother me. What bothers me are the things I understand, and don't do." How well that describes many Christians who don't live out their Christianity through their outward behavior.

The title and thrust of this book, *Deep Down*, comes from one of my favorite jokes:

> *Question:* Do you know why they bury lawyers twelve feet deep, instead of the usual six?
> *Answer:* Because deep down, they're good people.

Why is that joke humorous? Because all of us realize that whoever we are deep down will express itself in our behavior. Although we can fake behavior for a short time, our inside *will* reveal itself on the outside: "No good tree bears bad fruit, nor does a bad tree bear good fruit. Each tree is recognized by its own fruit. . . . The good man brings good things out of the good stored up in his heart, and the evil man brings evil things out of the evil stored up in his heart. For out of the overflow of his heart his mouth speaks" (Luke 6:43-45).

Most of us want to be different. We want to be godly. We want to obey. But we struggle with failure. We want to do the right thing, but it doesn't come easily. Obeying God goes against our grain.

How about you? Although you may not have lived a life like Mike's, have you ever sensed that God doesn't have a deep-down hold on your life? Have you sensed that you're not quite the same on the inside as you want to appear on the outside? Do you feel that although you truly want more of God, you're not sure what faith really is, let alone how to get it and hang on to it?

When people come to Christ, they often are told to *do* certain things in order to develop a solid faith: Go to church, read the Bible, stop doing this, and begin doing that. They're encouraged to tithe and to teach Sunday school.

But spirituality doesn't move from outward behavior inward. Spirituality begins on the *inside* and works its way *outside*. When it comes to true spirituality, the important thing is to let God get deep down within us, allowing him to transform us from the inside out.

Who we are deep down will always reveal itself in what we do. And after thirty-six years as a Christian and seventeen in ministry, I'm convinced many Christians don't change meaningfully at their conversion because they don't allow God to change their character deep down.

EXPERIENCING DEEP-DOWN CHARACTER CHANGE

When we come to Christ, changes take place, beginning in our innermost person and then spreading outward. But what changes are we talking about? What should we look like as we begin to reflect the character of God?

In this book we'll examine nine character traits that can change us into people who walk intimately with God and reflect his loving character. These traits include valuing people enough to get beyond our own self-centered concerns, discovering how to have deep-seated joy in the worst of difficulties and inner peace even in the fast lane, and more.

If you already want the absolute best God offers and if you want to be a new person in Christ, this book will give you clear, practical, and biblical direction on what it means to change your character.

If you aren't sure you want to get that involved in Christianity, this book will encourage you to step beyond your current level of faith into the exciting adventure and challenge of inner transformation that can change your life forever.

I know, because it changed mine.

SURFACE CHRISTIANITY

Heart-wrenching despair is still a fresh memory. I grew up in a churchgoing family, accepted Christ, and was baptized at age eleven. Before my senior year of high school in 1965, I attended summer camp. Emotions were incredibly high as we sang countless verses of "Just As I Am," and many of my close friends went to stand at the fire ring to indicate their commitment to Christ. The pressure was on. I finally joined them, giving "my life to full-time Christian service."

Even though my decision was basically sincere, I knew even then that some of my motivation was to get an extra good-night kiss from my camp sweetheart, Rosie, who had already decided to become a missionary.

I entered a Christian college to prepare for the ministry. But by the end of that first year, things had changed. I had done all I had been told to do to be a good Christian. But when confronted with the questions, temptations, and stresses of college life, even at a Christian college, that surface faith gave way to no faith.

My faith was based on what others said and was focused on surface behavior. Knowing I couldn't live up to what I knew was right led to four years of searching, questioning, and trying to discover truth. I still believed God existed, but I wasn't too sure who he was, much less what he wanted from me. Despite having some trust in Jesus' words in the Bible, I wasn't too sure about the other writers in it.

Although I didn't get involved in the excesses of those hippie days, I certainly had no assurance that if I died, I would meet God in heaven.

But on the surface, life in college went well. I was in graduate school, working as a grad assistant, getting good grades, living in an off-campus duplex with a friend. Life included a car, a motorcycle, and three girlfriends (none of them knew about the others, so I survived!). In my mind I had become a success.

Yet deep within I knew something was missing. My semi-dormant sense of right and wrong told me I needed to make some changes. At the top of the list was an innate self-centeredness I intensely disliked. Usually I hid it well. I learned the best way to get my way was not to look as if I wanted my way. If I appeared to give in on some inconsequential items, I could usually get the things I really wanted.

I lived life for me. The girlfriends were there to please me, not for me to meet their needs. I was nice enough to keep them around, but that was the limit. College professors were to be stroked for good grades, not befriended for any wisdom they might share.

But I didn't like who I was, and I tried to change that selfishness. Despite my best efforts, I failed. I couldn't avoid manipulating the women in my life. I knew better, tried to do better, did so for a short time, but ultimately failed. Up to that point, most things in my life had come fairly easy. I got nearly everything I truly wanted and went after. But try as I might, I couldn't change the inner me. I could make surface changes, but I couldn't change myself deep down. That failure devastated me. In February 1971 I was brought to despair. I considered suicide but rejected its permanency. I wandered the beach at night, searching for significance in the waves. Nothing helped.

During those years of searching, I discovered the tremendous historical evidence for Christianity and the reliability of the Bible. Those issues were settled. But I wasn't yet sure if Christianity would work in practice; it certainly hadn't worked for me before. Then, in just one month, God marvelously went to work. He wove together a *Marcus Welby* television show depicting a young blind man restored to sight by an operation. I despised his new self-centered behavior until I realized he was me. Next came a college conference at Mission Bay in San Diego, California. The theme was "Doing It," showing how Christians live their faith from the inside out. I was impressed by these Christians with integrity; they were the same on the inside as the outside.

The final touch was going "by chance" to a campus Bible study, where I picked up a small devotional booklet. Each page seemed to be written for me. Philippians 2:3-4 gave the goal: "Do nothing out of selfish ambition or vain conceit, but in humility consider others better than yourselves. Each of you should look not only to your own interests, but also to the interests of others." That balance was what I had always wanted. Then the solution came in Colossians 3:9-10: "Do not lie to each other, since you have taken off your old self with its practices and have *put on the new self,* which is being renewed in knowledge in the image of its Creator" (emphasis mine).

I was already motivated to change, and these verses provided the concrete examples and hope that change could be accomplished. But even more important, God revealed *how* to make the changes: I had to allow him to remake me into a new person. The final step in my pilgrimage was realizing that God wanted to change me and that he *could* do that.

God showed me reality, and it wasn't what I had been taught. Previously, Christianity had been a code of behavior (for example, "Christians don't smoke, drink, or go with girls who do"). But I found that Christianity is a life. It isn't so much a religion as a relationship with God, a relationship that changes the very core of one's being. My baptism in 1959 was done out of obedience because people and the Bible told me it was important. And it was. But I didn't realize then that baptism proclaims our transformation: "We were therefore buried with him through baptism into death in order that, just as Christ was raised from the dead through the glory of the Father, we too may *live a new life*" (Romans 6:4, emphasis mine).

As an early 1970s radical, I found something to get radical about—something worth giving myself to wholeheartedly. I had the awesome privilege of knowing the

Creator of the universe, personally. His Son promised to live within me. His Spirit could lead, guide, and strengthen me. Even more valuable, he could make me into the person I knew I should be. Later that night, I knelt by my bed and surrendered my life to God: "God, if you can make anything out of this life, do it. You've got complete freedom to make any changes you desire. I need you."

Overnight, my life was transformed; who I was changed. I wasn't even aware of some of the changes until others pointed them out, usually with great relief and joy.

I still remember a debate team member saying, "Tim, I don't know what's happened, but you're different. Before, when we drove to a tournament, you would look out the window, get lost in yourself, even look at your reflection in the sideview mirror. But now you converse with compassion. You care about others — and it shows."

I thought they hadn't noticed! The embarrassment at realizing others saw those old patterns was humiliating. But such comments taught me that inner character changes were already working their way to the outside.

I became addicted. The joy of overcoming the first entrenched sin pattern set the stage for wanting more. I wanted deeper character changes. This life process has been a struggle; not all months produce startling success. Although I'm not yet where I passionately want to be, I'm further along than I was in February 1971, when God began recreating my life.

RADICAL CHANGE IS NEEDED

Make no mistake: God loves us as we are. But he also loves us too much to let us remain as we are. God wants us to become a new person on the inside, and the changes required are deep down. Obviously, our identity remains the same, but those character changes lead to such extensive changes in our values, our mind, our emotions, and our behavior that we do become a new person. The following verses describe the extent of how God wants us to change us (emphasis mine):

Therefore, we do not lose heart. Though outwardly we are wasting away, yet *inwardly we are being renewed* day by day. (2 Corinthians 4:16)

Therefore, if anyone is in Christ, he is a *new creation;* the old has gone, the new has come! (2 Corinthians 5:17)

Put on *the new self,* created to be like God in true righteousness and holiness. (Ephesians 4:24)

Praise be to the God and Father of our Lord Jesus Christ! In his great mercy he has *given us new birth* into a living hope through the resurrection of Jesus Christ from the dead. (1 Peter 1:3)

Coming to Christ brings such a radical change deep down that we're called a new person. That's what it means to be born again. Jesus gave a very clear reason why we need to change so dramatically when he talked about wineskins in Matthew 9:17.

In the first century, new wine was put into new, unused leather skins. The wine was young and strong, still active with its natural fermentation. New skins were flexible and strong, able to contain the powerful new wine. But over time, as the fermentation process stopped and the wine lost its pop, the skins also lost their flexibility. Just as old wine suited old skins, new wine suited new skins. Those early winemakers learned never to put new wine into old skins: "Neither do men pour new wine into old wineskins. If they do, the skins will burst, the wine will run out, and the wineskins will be ruined. No, they pour new wine into new wineskins, and both are preserved."

Although Jesus was an excellent winemaker (see what he did at the wedding feast in Cana, in John 2:1-10), he wasn't talking about wine. Wineskins picture who we are inside; the new wine reflects the active Holy Spirit, who lives within us when we become a Christian. Our lives need to be new to contain the purity and power of God. If we try to fit the Holy Spirit into our old lives, without a deep-down transformation, we'll explode in frustration.

Perhaps that's why so many cults who strongly stress proper behavior have such high numbers of suicides, teenage problems, and marriage difficulties. People just can't live up to the rigorous behavioral demands. The true power of God doesn't live within them, so they cannot be transformed as a person from the inside out. As frustration grows in their lives, it is manifested in outward behavior. The basic cause: They're not able to become new skins on the inside in order to handle the pressures of difficult obedience requirements.

God makes it clear that walking with him requires a deep-down change of our character. Change is essential to Christianity. But how do we begin that process of change? That's what we'll discuss in the next chapter.

STEPS TOWARD CHARACTER CHANGE
1. Do you think we should change our ways to become Christians or that we should come to Christ and let him change our ways? Explain your answer.

2. Some people accept Christ and join a local church but never seem to change much. What would you say to such a person?

3. Put the following Scripture passages into your own words:
   - Romans 6:4
   - Romans 12:2
   - 2 Corinthians 4:16
   - 2 Corinthians 5:17
   - Ephesians 4:24
   - Colossians 3:9-10
   - 1 Peter 1:3

   What do these verses say to you personally about character change?

4. What do you think is your best spiritual feature? Your worst?

5. Share your decision to cooperate with God in deep-down character change with someone you trust. Ask that person to pray for you and to hold you accountable for making needed changes.

CHAPTER 2

A Roadmap for Change

During the Civil War, President Lincoln attended a Wednesday evening service at a church close to the White House. Accompanied by his Secret Service agents, Lincoln would sit in the pastor's study during the message; then they would walk back together. One evening, after the service, an agent asked Lincoln, "What did you think of tonight's sermon?"

Lincoln replied, "It was brilliantly conceived, biblical, relevant, and well presented."

"So, it was a great sermon?"

"No, it failed. It failed because Dr. Gurley did not ask us to do something great."

Inspiration without application merely breeds frustration. If we believe character change is vital to the Christian life but don't have a roadmap to get there, our time is wasted.

HOW DO WE CHANGE?

What is the source of our power to change? Do we rely on our own ability, or does God make the changes?

Transformation through Partnership

On the one hand, if we believe that "man is master of his own fate" and rely on our own willpower to change, we discover the most discouraging form of impotence in making deep-down changes. On the other hand, if we believe that God does it all and we are only bystanders, we become passive.

Both assumptions are true in affirming the key role of one of the players in this action, but they err in denying that the second player has a role. What does the Bible say about our role and God's role in character change? Philippians 2:12-13 beautifully expresses the balance: "Therefore, my dear friends, as you have always obeyed—not only in my presence, but now much more in my absence—*continue to work out* your salvation with fear and trembling, for it is *God who works in you* to will and to act according to his good purpose" (emphasis mine).

Did you notice the duality: that we work *and* that God works? Significantly, Paul chooses two different Greek words for our single English word *work*. Paul used *katergazomai* for our work. *Vine's Expository Dictionary* describes it as "to work out, achieve, effect by toil." But for God's work, Paul uses *energeo*, defined by *Vine's* as "to work in, to be active, operative." Both ways of working combine efforts and results, but notice the direction of work: God works in; we work out.

Let's use the example of a physical workout. Working out with weights won't give us muscles we don't have. God's creative work places muscles in us. But our working out strengthens and develops what we've been given. The degree of our strength directly relates to how much we work out.

The principle of working out in Christianity is the same. Our salvation has been given to us through Christ's finished work on the cross. But we need to work that salvation out into each area of our lives. We also need to cooperate with God in a partnership to incorporate his character into us.

On the surface, these statements seem to contradict each other. Who does the work—do we or does God? But the paradox of our spiritual partnership is that *both* work together. Spiritual transformation isn't a simplistic formula but a mysterious and complex interaction between God and a person. Some things only we can do; some things only God can do; some things we'll both be involved with. But throughout, we cooperate with God in the transformation.

How do we work with God in that process? The beginning point in developing Christian character is our will.

A Decision of Our Will

As Donald Guthrie said in his *New Testament Theology,* "No ethic [character trait] can be imposed on an obstinate will. . . . This [developing a Christian ethic or character] cannot happen except by individual willingness to surrender."

Our will begins the process of transformation. We value having God's character, and we decide to start the process. Sometimes God, fully on his own, will then make major character changes within us. My self-centered ways left overnight without any involvement on my part except to ask for it.

Other times, character changes will involve a slow, painful, working out. Our decision of the will is followed by concrete actions on our part, where we work on that trait until it becomes embedded within us. God provides the power; we provide the doing. Sometimes these two methods are combined. God will start the process by making a major change. We then continue to work out that change.

19

But transformation requires a partnership: our will coupled with God's power. We take the first step of wanting to change our character in conjunction with God. Then God steps in and provides whatever we lack. God will not change us without our involvement; we cannot change ourselves without his involvement.

WHERE DO WE CHANGE?

We think about changes in three major areas: our behavior, our personality, and our character (see Figure 1).

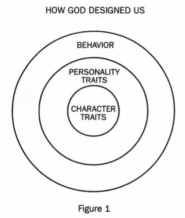

HOW GOD DESIGNED US

Figure 1

Behavior

We've all seen "godly" people whose lives suddenly self-destruct spiritually. Like Mike in chapter 1, many people "try" Christianity by attempting to adopt a code of behavior. But they tend to give up, saying, "It just didn't work for me." Everyone can fake "good Christian" behavior, at least for a time. But what we are inside will eventually come out.

These failings usually result from trying to change the wrong part first. Behavior is important. Moral guilt or virtue are closely linked to our actions. But we don't *begin* the process of change with our behavior. Rather, we cooperate with God to change our inner person, and then we see the results of that change in our behavior.

God wants our actions to be the fruit of a changed life. He doesn't first of all look for behavior changes.

Personality

God also doesn't look for our primary changes to happen in our personality traits. Although behavior, personality, and character are linked, they have tremendous differences. Personality is the raw material of our inner person, a complex blend of traits. We can be shy or outgoing, talkative or quiet, submissive or dominant, a leader or a follower. God created us with a mix of traits that make us unique.

Although when we become Christians we will change in some personality areas, usually we won't experience a wholesale personality makeover. Personality can be compared to our body. If we're born with genes that make us five-and-a-half feet tall, we'll never be a seven-foot center in the National Basketball Association.

We can stretch ourselves on a rack, eat all the proper foods, practice jumping, but we'll reach seven feet only when we stand on a ladder. We can improve our body, but we just don't get beyond our natural boundaries.

Our personality traits are similar. God works *with* our basic personality, not against it. When God wants to make us over in his image, he's not primarily out to change our personality. He wants character transformation.

Character

What is character? *Moral excellence or firmness.* Character is the person we are deep down, when nobody is looking. Character is the mix of inner qualities that determine who we are: our values, and our determination to act on those values. Moral guilt or moral excellence are most closely linked to our character. Since character is internal, people don't see it directly. Instead, they see the ways in which our character expresses itself through actions.

The good news is that character can change. When God

21

creates a new person, his work touches character, and the result is changed behavior. In fact, behavior is the expression of character through personality. Let's explore how these three areas—character, personality, and behavior—interrelate (see Figure 2).

HOW CHARACTER TRAITS WORK

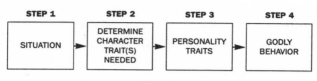

Figure 2

In step 1 we encounter a problem or situation that requires response.

In step 2 we determine how to respond, based on our motives. Motives are closely aligned with our character, and we have a wide range to choose from. For instance, I operated for my first twenty-three years with motives like, "People tell me a good Christian should do this" and "What's most to my benefit?" Other motives could be, "I want people to see me this way" or "I've always done it this way." We bring our Christian character traits into the process when we determine which trait or traits are most appropriate.

In step 3 we run our motives, or character, through the vehicle of our blend of personality traits.

Step 4 is the result—godly behavior, or what we do to show our most deep-seated motives, through the unique matrix of our personality.

That four-step process can be traced through any situation, with any character trait, through any personality trait, resulting in the most appropriate godly behavior for that unique individual. Let's examine how an engaged couple,

Bill and Megan, who are deeply committed to God, confronted the same situation: sexual temptation.

Bill is a quiet, rather submissive guy who normally goes along with whatever Megan wants to do. Megan has a strong, assertive personality and usually takes the initiative in setting boundaries. But on the occasions when Megan struggles and doesn't really want to set limits, Bill's character trait of purity overcomes his natural submissiveness, and he steps in to establish boundaries.

Bill and Megan faced the same situation, had the same motives, but their unique personalities resulted in different forms of godly behavior. And this is true for everyone. Each individual begins with character and then uniquely expresses that character through personality in godly behavior.

In the Christian life, the key battleground is our character, our inner person, our inner values, our inner firmness, our inner courage. Until we allow God to change us from the inside out through our character, our behavior won't be consistently different. But once we allow God to change our character, deep down, then we can have consistently godly behavior.

CHANGING FROM THE INSIDE OUT

Changing our character begins within, from the decision of our will to cooperate with God to be remade into his image. Listen to what the apostle Paul commanded in Romans 12:1-2: "Therefore, I urge you, brothers, in view of God's mercy, to offer your bodies as living sacrifices, holy and pleasing to God—this is your spiritual act of worship. Do not conform any longer to the pattern of this world, but be transformed by the renewing of your mind."

What is Paul saying? Give yourself fully to God. Don't

hold anything back. That's what worship is. As J. B. Phillips said in his version, "Don't let the world around you squeeze you into its own mould, but let God re-make you so that your whole attitude of mind is changed."

How is that transformation, that "re-making" to occur? By a change of our minds. We decide we want to give all of ourselves to God so that he can make us into the person he designed us to be.

But the choosing is a part of the partnership. God won't force us. But our merely making a choice won't accomplish the change either. That's what I learned during my painful time of despair in 1971. I knew what changes were necessary, and I wanted to make them, but I didn't have the power within myself.

Developing Christian character traits requires that working partnership between us and God. Our role is to want those changes, to allow God to do what's necessary, and to work out what God's working in. God's role is to live within us, to incarnate his character into ours. We provide the decision; God provides the power. Both are essential for the character changes to transpire. The key to this process is to understand the concept of the fruit of the Spirit.

UNDERSTANDING THE FRUIT OF THE SPIRIT

Galatians 5:16-26 marvelously details what it means to have God's character grow within us. The goal is given in verses 22-23: "But the fruit of the Spirit is love, joy, peace, patience, kindness, goodness, faithfulness, gentleness and self-control. Against such things there is no law."

Each aspect of the fruit of the Spirit represents a specific trait of God's character, which we'll examine, one trait per chapter, in the next nine chapters of this book. When God lives within us through his Spirit, his character transfers itself to ours. And as we allow his Spirit to remake each aspect of our lives, God's character becomes embedded in ours and increasingly expresses itself in our character traits.

Once again, it takes the paradox of partnering with God to become new persons who express the fruit of the Spirit. A gardener doesn't cause fruit, such as apples, to form, and the tree doesn't produce apples merely by deciding it will. But a healthy apple tree produces apples because the fruit is part of its nature, an expression of its physical genes. In the same way, Christian character traits, the fruit of the Spirit, express our spiritual genes.

When we're healthy Christians, indwelt and led by the Spirit, we'll express the fruit of the Spirit. When we allow God's Spirit to cultivate, weed, feed, and water us for maximum health, we'll have deep-down character changes that reflect the character of God (see Figure 3).

HOW CHARACTER TRAITS ARE DEVELOPED

STEP 1	STEP 2	STEP 3	STEP 4
DESIRE GOD'S CHARACTER	CULTIVATE YOUR RELATIONSHIP WITH GOD	WEED OUT OBSTACLES	NURTURE EACH TRAIT

Figure 3

Step 1 in developing godly character traits involves our will. We decide to have God's character transplanted into us. To attain this, we must want God passionately, to desire him above all else in life.

In Galatians 5:16-17 Paul teaches that our lives will express *either* our original sinful nature or the Spirit living within:

> So I say, *live by the Spirit,* and you will not gratify the desires of the sinful nature. For the sinful nature de-

sires what is contrary to the Spirit, and the Spirit what is contrary to the sinful nature. *They are in conflict* with each other, so that you do not do what you want. (emphasis mine).

Specific acts are not what most concerned Paul, but the source of those acts.

Do we allow our original character, not shaped by God, to direct our lives? Or do we allow the Holy Spirit to live within us, changing our values, commitments, and essence? These are decisions each of us must make every day.

Step 2 in developing Christian character traits is to nourish the source of our life, our root: in essence, to "live by the Spirit." We nurture our spiritual life as we let God live in us through his Spirit and as we follow his leading. As a help for learning more about allowing God to live in us, I recommend two excellent books: *Knowing God* by J. I. Packer and *The Knowledge of the Holy* by A. W. Tozer. This book will focus on two remaining steps, examining how each specific trait develops within us.

Step 3 deals with eliminating in our lives anything that is inconsistent with Christian character. We face great danger in trying to fit God into our lives if we don't fully want to give up our old, sinful nature:

The acts of the sinful nature are obvious: sexual immorality, impurity and debauchery; idolatry and witchcraft; hatred, discord, jealousy, fits of rage, selfish ambition, dissensions, factions and envy; drunkenness, orgies, and the like. I warn you, as I did before, that those who live like this *will not inherit* the kingdom of God. (Galatians 5:19-21, emphasis mine)

26

Many of us avoid the more glaring sins in that list. But do we continually bicker with a brother? Does our temper sometimes flare out of control? Have we broken the church into separate groups fighting for supremacy? Do we envy another's musical talent? These are symptoms of the sinful nature expressing itself in our behavior.

Notice the clear warning in verse 21. Writing to members of the church, to people who were at least nominal Christians, Paul said that if these acts characterize our lives, we won't inherit the kingdom of God. Does this mean we have to do good things to earn our salvation? Not at all. Paul is just making it clear to us that if these acts characterize our lives, our inner character is still dominated by the original sinful nature. We haven't allowed God to change our character, our inner person. We're putting new wine into the old skins of our lives. And if we're doing this, our lives will self-destruct spiritually when surface behavioral changes meet the spiritual crises of life. To develop God's character traits, we need to weed out our spiritual garden from the acts of our old sinful nature.

Once we've begun to weed our spiritual garden, we then need step 4: to nurture each trait consciously. We need to feed, fertilize, prune, and thin our fruit for maximum fruitfulness. In upcoming chapters we'll look at the specifics for nurturing each trait. For now, understand that nurturing is part of the process of living by the Spirit and allowing the Spirit to develop our lives as he desires. Both play a vital function in partnership.

PARTNERING WITH
GOD TAKES COMMITMENT
To the extent that we limit the deep-down work of God in

us, we limit the deep-down character we have. To the extent that we give God freedom in our lives, we'll experience the freedom to develop these traits. But when we don't allow God to work within our inner person, we become a wild, uncultivated fruit tree, with little fruit.

In the early decades of the twentieth century, the Owens Valley in the eastern High Sierras was a fertile farming region. Just south of the town of Independence, an apple orchard was planted next to Shepherd's Creek. The combination of rich soil, winter cold, and sparkling stream water for irrigation produced apples that won blue ribbons in many fairs and that were shipped all over the country.

But the water rights to most of the valley were obtained by the city of Los Angeles to slake the thirst of their growing development. Without water, the orchard was neglected, receiving only winter snows and infrequent summer rains. No pruning was done to remove unwanted growth. No fertilizing was done to enhance vitality. For a while the orchard stubbornly held on. When my father and I began fishing together in the late 1950s, one tradition was to stop and pick apples from that orchard. Though the apples were few in number, their taste was great. We made applesauce over an open fire, spicing it with cinnamon.

Today the orchard is gone. Continued neglect eventually took its toll. The trees finally quit producing fruit, died, and were removed.

As Christians, we won't bear the fruit of the Spirit—love, joy, peace, patience, kindness, goodness, faithfulness, gentleness, and self-control—unless we're under cultivation by the Spirit. If we neglect that cultivation, we become like that apple orchard in the Owens Valley. Fruitless.

What about you? How committed are you to allowing the cultivation process in your life?

In the remainder of this book, we'll learn how to develop the character of God deep down, so that others see the result. Each of the next nine chapters will examine a fruit of the Spirit. We'll begin by looking at our natural tendency regarding each character trait, then we'll define the trait and give examples of how that trait is seen in the character of God. Next, we'll look at the two-stage process of cultivating the trait and weeding out any behaviors that work against the development of that trait. Then we'll pursue ways in which we can nurture that trait in our everyday lives. Each chapter will end with questions and thought-provoking ideas that will encourage you as you step toward character change.

STEPS TOWARD CHARACTER CHANGE

1. What is the difference between character, personality, and behavior? Which is the hardest to change? Explain.
2. Why is trying to change from the outside in not a good idea? Give scriptural backing for your answer, if possible.
3. Which do you think is the most difficult: to weed out anything inconsistent with Christian character or to nurture the fruit of the Spirit?
4. If you have ever felt the need to change, what did you do about it? If you tried to change yourself, did you fail or succeed? How did that make you feel? What has happened subsequently?
5. In Galatians 5:16-26 we're told to "live by the Spirit." What does that phrase mean to you?
6. What role does wanting God passionately have in developing Christian character traits?
7. Discuss the connection of fruit with character.

In what ways can we interfere with God in the development of good character?

8. Of the nine fruit of the Spirit in Galatians 5:22-23–love, joy, peace, patience, kindness, goodness, faithfulness, gentleness, self-control— which do you feel is the most developed trait in your life? Which is the least developed?

9. Which parts of changing your character are apt to be most difficult?

10. Talk to someone you trust about the part(s) of your character you feel will be most difficult to change. Ask that person to pray for you and to suggest specific ways in which he or she can assist you in making the needed change(s).

PART TWO

Nine Christian Character Traits

CHAPTER 3

Getting beyond Ourselves

Love

But the fruit of the Spirit is love. . . .
— PAUL THE APOSTLE, in GALATIANS 5:22

My dad was both my role model and my greatest rival, particularly on fishing trips. Despite our friendly competition, I learned a lot about "thinking like a trout" from the expert. To this day, I've not seen anyone match Dad on a trout stream. After years of fishing together, I finally was able to come close to matching him when fishing was decent. But even when the trout had little interest in biting, he kept pulling them out. I never was able to match him.

Our bonding on fishing trips increased through our competition to catch the most trout, and the largest. That was why, on a late fall trip to the Sierras when I was sixteen, I wanted to land a huge trout so badly. As I drifted a worm along an undercut bank on Oak Creek, the line stopped. Since I couldn't feel a tug on the line cradled between my thumb and forefinger to indicate a bite, I pulled the line out of the water to try again. But it just stayed there. I gave a yank, thinking it was snagged on a root.

Slowly the "root" gave way, with the largest trout head I had ever seen breaking the surface before it let go. The head alone seemed as big as most trout. My heart stopped; my body quivered. Gradually I composed myself, waited a few moments for the trout to settle down, and floated the line past the hole again. But this time the line kept moving. That worm was well drowned before I acknowledged this trout was through biting.

Hours later, Dad and I came back to the spot, and I described the whale of a trout. Once again I put my line into the hole. "Tim, you didn't get a bite," Dad said, chuckling from the other side of the stream. "Your line is hung up on a root. You're not even in the water."

Dad was right about the root but wrong about the fish. Just seconds later a rainbow trout erupted from the hole, bending my fly rod double. Once he was over the bank, I pounced. That guy wasn't going to fall back in. He was sixteen inches of beauty, weighing in at one and a half pounds. Huge for a stream just four feet wide, he was even bigger for a young man eager to prove himself as a true fisherman to his dad. I was filled with pride and accomplishment. I had never seen even Dad catch one this big in a stream.

The euphoria lasted into the next day as we moved south to another creek. We were fishing twenty feet apart when Dad cautiously took his line out and called me over. "There's a nice one in there. He quit biting for me, but maybe you can get him. Just let your line drop over the waterfall, and he'll strike when it hits the surface, if he's going to."

I slipped into place. Letting out just three feet of line, the worm went over the falls. *Bam.* Another big one. This one measured just a little less than the first, fifteen and a half inches and just a little under one and a half pounds.

Knowing Dad's competitive nature and fishing prowess,

I was suspicious. "I bet you knew this guy was just a little smaller, and you didn't want to miss catching the largest fish by so little, did you?"

Dad smilingly denied it, but for years I teased him for giving up such a nice trout. It was only after his death, years later, that I finally realized what he had done.

Yes, Dad knew it was a big one. He couldn't help but know that. And no, the fish didn't quit biting for him. As soon as my worm hit the water, that fish struck hard. He was hungry. He would have bitten on anything.

But Dad knew the trout was a big one, maybe bigger than mine from the day before. And he didn't want to risk catching a bigger trout than his son's catch of a lifetime. Dad offered a tremendous act of love, unappreciated for years, until it was too late to acknowledge.

Actions like my dad's are difficult for most of us. Sacrificial giving goes against our grain. God calls for that kind of giving love, getting beyond ourselves. Not many people do that easily.

OUR NATURAL TENDENCY: SELF-ABSORPTION

After years of training and experience, a pastor left the ministry to practice medicine, saying, "People will pay more money to care for their bodies than their souls." After several more years he made another career change, this time to the legal profession. His reasoning? "People will pay more to get their own way than they will to take care of either body or soul."

That story reveals not only the pastor's motives but also the motives of many people. We tend to look at life through our perspective: I'm persistent, but you're pigheaded; I'm convinced, but you're stubborn; I'm flexible, but you're wishy-washy. If our needs were placed on a balance scale at the opposite end from our concerns for others, the slant toward self would be severe.

Although we all have done some selfless acts, we still tend to look at life mostly through the filter of "What's best for me?" Marketing people recognize our innate selfishness and reinforce that nature by unneeded encouragements to "Have it *your way,*" "You *deserve* a break today," and "Who said you can't *have it all?*" Why do they stress such attitudes? They've learned we respond. Those statements resonate with something deep within us.

The apostle Paul recognized our continual struggle with that innate trait. Writing to Christians nearly two thousand years ago, he said, "For everyone looks out for his own interests, not those of Jesus Christ" (Philippians 2:21). Humanity hasn't improved much in the last two millennia. We still battle the desire for preeminence, power, and position.

Read through the Gospels to learn how often the disciples argued over who was greatest. When Jesus caught them, they showed appropriate embarrassment, but they still continued in their debate until the very end of Jesus' ministry. Even at the Last Supper, Peter boasted that he alone would remain true to Christ. To Peter, Peter was the best disciple.

Each of us sees that same trait in our own hearts. We have scattered victories, but we all tend to be possessed with self. Our desires are at the forefront of our minds.

THE CHRISTIAN CHARACTER TRAIT OF LOVE
How does our Christianity impact that innate trait of self-concern when God's character becomes embedded in ours?

Because the issue of self-centeredness is so pivotal to our Christian walk, the first area in which God usually transforms us is in getting beyond ourselves. We must learn to balance our own genuine needs with compassion for others. Why else would love — God's antidote to selfishness — be listed as the first expression of the character of God within? When God comes into our lives, we finally have both the motivation and power to get beyond our preoccupation with our own concerns. And it's all wrapped up in the character trait of love.

Love Defined

What is love? Our society seems to define it as "a feeling." You can love chocolate, love a puppy, or love a person. But is that the love God wants to incorporate in us? Certainly not. God's love can be defined more like this: "Love is an inner valuing of another, a valuing that causes you to act in the best interests of the person you love."

First of all, love is a deep-seated character trait that comes from our attitude about the person we love. That person's value isn't based on lovableness or sinless perfection but on the fact that God loves and values him or her.

That inner commitment isn't a feeling. Feelings come and go, based on our hormone levels, how much sleep we got the night before, and the person's last behavior toward us. Love based on feelings is a roller-coaster ride with great highs, great lows, and always a great deal of fear mixed with exhilaration.

The inner character of love values others as much as ourselves. This results in specific, intentional action that is based on what's best for others spiritually, emotionally, and physically. In other words, we commit ourselves to helping them be who God designed them to be. We don't cave in to all their desires. We don't allow them to escape responsibility for their decisions. But we interrupt our self-centered agenda, get beyond self-absorption, and become a positive influence in their lives.

God's Love

God loves by acting for our best: "But God demonstrates his own love for us in this: While we were still sinners, Christ died for us" (Romans 5:8). While we were sinners (certainly not deserving of great love), God acted out of his inner character of love (it had to be demonstrated to be known) by sending his Son to die for us (observable, practical action for our spiritual benefit). Because love filled God's character, he acted for our best, at his own cost: "For God so loved the world that he gave his one and only Son, that whoever believes in him shall not perish but have eternal life" (John 3:16).

These verses say nothing about God's feelings toward us. If you combine his holiness with our repeated sinfulness, God's feelings could very well have been disgust, anger, and disappointment. But feelings don't drive God. His inner love does. Because God loves, he acts. And he encourages us to love the same way—with actions, not with feelings— in 1 Corinthians 13:4-8: "Love is patient, love is kind. It does not envy, it does not boast, it is not proud. It is not rude, it is not self-seeking, it is not easily angered, it keeps no record of wrongs. Love does not delight in evil but rejoices with the truth. It always protects, always trusts, always hopes, always perseveres. Love never fails."

Love is embedded in God's character. All he does flows from love. For us to learn what love is, we need to commit ourselves to the study of God. This chapter provides a start on learning how God acts toward people.

The Bible is the world's best manual on love because in it, we see how love flows from God's character into his behavior. I encourage you to spend some time, as you're reading your Bible, looking for that very thing. Discover the extent of God's love: How many people can receive it? Notice the depth: How far is God willing to go in his love? Determine the actions of love: What does God do to demonstrate his love? Uncover how his love ends: that nothing we can do will keep God from loving us.

Some passages are obvious—for example, 1 Corinthians 13, also known as the love chapter, and 1 John, where in five brief chapters a form of the word *love* is used approximately forty-six times. But don't miss less obvious passages, like Genesis chapters 1–3. Find the wonderful gift of Eden, then marvel at the love that prompted the promise of a Redeemer to overcome the effects of man choosing sin. Examine the story of God calling Abram, in Genesis 12, revealing God's desire that "all peoples on earth will be blessed"—not just the chosen Jews, but all. Study the book of Judges, where God's people frequently left and betrayed him, but in love he always was there when they turned around. A good, exhaustive concordance would be helpful for even further study as you learn how the God who lives within us loves.

As we understand more fully how God loves, we can begin to incorporate the trait of love into our own character.

CULTIVATING LOVE

The greatest obstacle to love is the natural self-absorption that says our needs, fears, desires, and preferences come first. Just look at "innocent infants." You can't find more selfish creatures; the world revolves around them. But as they grow, they're supposed to learn how valuable others are, to learn to balance concern for themselves with concern for others. That's the way God designed us.

Even as sinners, we have an innate value God recognizes (Romans 5:8), and we need to recognize that same value in others. A person's value doesn't come from behavior because no one can be good enough for a pure God to love on the basis of behavior. Liking usually comes from traits or behavior in others. We tend to *like* people who are likable, who are like us, who do good things for us. But we *love* people because they are people, not because of their worthiness. People need love, and we need to give love:

> You have heard that it was said, "Love your neighbor and hate your enemy." But I tell you: Love your enemies and pray for those who persecute you, that you may be sons of your Father in heaven. He causes his sun to rise on the evil and the good, and sends rain on the righteous and the unrighteous. If you love those who love you, what reward will you get? Are not even the tax collectors doing that? And if you greet only your brothers, what are you doing more than others? Do not even pagans do that? Be perfect, therefore, as your heavenly Father is perfect. (Matthew 5:43-48)

Jesus strongly connected our becoming children of God and our loving the unlovely, including those who bring us distress. That means we take concrete action on their behalf. Why is that so important? Because that's God's character, and he wants his children to be like him.

We need to cultivate an awareness of the innate value all people have. The first step in that cultivation process involves weeding out certain attitudes and actions that can choke out the growth of love.

Weeding Out Selfishness and Selective Love

Two basic weeds that work against developing love are the weed of selfishness and the weed of selective or partial love.

The Weed of Selfishness. First of all, we must recognize that basic preoccupation with self is part of our sinful nature and that we can never completely eliminate our concern for ourselves because God gave that concern as a means of self-protection. But we do need to weed out the attitude of selfishness that dominates us. According to Philippians 2:3-8, when we balance our innate concern for ourselves with a care for others, we weed out selfishness:

> *Do nothing out of selfish ambition* or vain conceit, but in humility consider others better than yourselves. Each of you should look *not only* to your own interests, *but also* to the interests of others. Your attitude should be the same as that of Christ Jesus: Who, being in very nature God, did not consider equality with God something to be grasped, but made himself nothing, taking the very nature of a servant, being made in human likeness. And being found in appearance as a man, he humbled himself and became obedient to death—even death on a cross! (emphasis mine)

How do we overcome our innate selfishness? By adding an active concern for others. Loving others doesn't mean we completely ignore our own valid needs and interests. But we develop a balance. We look after our interests, *and* we look after the interests of others. We escape the trap of self-centeredness. When Christ lives in us, he reveals his character in and through us. We become loving because we're a child of God.

It's so easy for us to get out of balance. Some people are

so self-absorbed that they never even see the neediness of others. Their lives are dedicated to "looking out for number one." Other people are too self-sacrificing. They ignore their own valid needs out of a misbegotten idea of what love is, thinking, *If it gives me pleasure, it must be wrong.* They sacrifice genuine needs and soon burn out.

We must never forget that our needs are important. True needs are needs; they're nonnegotiable. We must look after them, but they alone can't drive our lives. Others have needs too, some that only we can satisfy. As we actively build concern for others and look for concrete ways to express our love, we weed out our innate selfishness. God develops his character in us, and we become like him: loving in all we do.

The Weed of Selective or Partial Love. One of the greatest threats to developing love is the weed of selective or partial love. For instance, we make some progress in becoming more loving and take justifiable pride in it. Although we don't love everyone, we have learned to love some people more deeply. Or we may love many people, even though we don't love anyone deeply.

We may think we've mastered the trait of love, but partial love isn't enough. Surface love can sidetrack us from getting love deep down into our character. We love in part when we love those who are easy to love, who love us. And we justify not loving others with rational reasons that they don't deserve love or that we do love them some. But that's not God's kind of love; his character trait of love extends to all people.

While talking to enlisted men on a U.S. Navy ship, a visiting admiral asked one of them, "What would you do if another sailor fell overboard?"

The enlisted man promptly replied, "I would raise the alarm and toss him a life preserver, sir."

The admiral then asked, "What would you do if it were an officer?"

At this, the sailor paused and thought before replying, "Which one, sir?"

Our tendency is to love those like us. But when God's love fills our being, we have a godly compassion for all people—not just those we like and identify with. We gain that compassion when we recognize the innate, God-given value every person has. Then we can feel some of their pain: "Rejoice with those who rejoice; mourn with those who mourn" (Romans 12:15). We begin to identify with others through our shared brokenness.

How do we weed out selective love? We begin the process by thinking and acting toward all people as we know God would act. We must value each person equally, as God does, and act in love toward everyone. This means we don't predominantly look on others as an audience. We'll want to get beyond trivial conversations to draw out other people's opinions, to discover what God is doing in them. And we work on doing this with *all* people. Why? Because we realize that love cannot be selective. It must be given fully to all.

NURTURING THE FRUIT OF LOVE

Just as we eliminate anything that works against godly love, so we need to deliberately nurture what will enhance love. We need to nurture the attitude that places a high value on loving others consistently.

The Value of Love

Love is the focal point where all aspects of faith come together. All we are and do flows from love. Jesus made that clear in Matthew 22:37-40 when he was asked about the greatest commandment: "'Love the Lord your God with all your heart and with all your soul and with all your mind.' This is the first and greatest commandment. And the second is like it: *'Love your neighbor* as yourself.' All the Law and the Prophets hang on these two commandments" (emphasis mine).

Jesus went beyond the original question about the greatest commandment because the second-greatest commandment couldn't be separated from the first. He taught that all important changes depend on loving God and loving one another.

When we allow God's character to shape ours, we become the person God designed us to be. We express God. All that we are should flow from the love of God within us: "For in Christ Jesus neither circumcision nor uncircumcision has any value. The only thing that counts is *faith expressing itself through love"* (Galatians 5:6, emphasis mine).

By itself, what we do has no value in pleasing God (a difficult concept for some of us who were taught that if we just do the right things, we'll please God). But as we realize how vital love is and begin to nurture it, we will please God by developing his character. We will begin to value the trait of love more than pleasing ourselves. We will consciously think, *How can I best express the love of God in this situation?* To achieve that, we must nurture our awareness of God's presence in us, because love flows from his character.

God's Love in Us

By nature, some people love more easily than others. But none of us loves as we should. The only way we can truly love from our character is when God is within us: "And hope does not disappoint us, because God has *poured out his love into our hearts* by the Holy Spirit, whom he has given us" (Romans 5:5, emphasis mine).

The Christian character trait of love doesn't come from our own natural, inborn ability to love. If so, many of us could never love. But God gives us part of his character, the ability to love: "And so we know and rely on the love God has for us. *God is love.* Whoever lives in love lives in God, and God in him" (1 John 4:16, emphasis mine).

The very essence of God is love. God can't act unlovingly because that action would violate who he is. And if that loving God is in us, then love is in us.

> How great is the love the Father has *lavished* on us, that we should be called children of God! And that is what we are! The reason the world does not know us is that it did not know him. Dear friends, now we are children of God, and what we will be has not yet been made known. But we know that when he appears, we shall *be like him,* for we shall see him as he is. (1 John 3:1-2, emphasis mine)

God has already lavished love on us—past tense. It has already been done. He gave us the tremendous privilege of being his children. Whatever this last verse says about our spiritual bodies, our role and duties in heaven, we do know we will be like him.

The love God has poured into us will reach its completion in heaven, but that love starts on earth. As soon as Christ comes to live within us, we take on his character. And since love flows from God by nature, when we allow God to express himself in us, we'll see love flowing from our lives. Even if our natural character is filled with envy, discord, selfishness, hatred, and anger, God can change all that. The love of God will transform the nature of a believer's "tree."

We can't love on our own; we must let God love

through us. And we don't gradually just *act* lovingly, we *become* more loving deep down. Love becomes embedded in our life as a fruit of the Spirit. But we can't be passive in the process and let God do all the work; it also takes training on our part.

Love Training

In 1 Timothy 4:7, the apostle Paul told his protégé Timothy, "Train yourself to be godly." How do we do that? An athlete trains by doing the proper thing over and over, until it becomes a habit. But practice doesn't make *perfect;* it only makes *permanent* whatever it is we practice.

It all begins with having God's love within, desiring it to permeate our character, then acting out loving behavior. So, in any situation, before we act, we need to ask ourselves, *According to God, what's the most loving thing to do? What can I do to make life better for this person, to help him or her grow spiritually?*

When people are exceptionally difficult to love, we must ask, *How can I best express God's love to this person?* Though we struggle honestly to love that person, looking at him or her through God's eyes will give us a greater desire to channel God's love to them through us.

Once we determine the most loving act, we choose to act, and continue to act in love, not from fickle feelings, but from a deep-down desire for that person's best.

The Cost of Love

This choice to act in love will often carry a cost, such as our time, finances, or pride. As we walk along with God in our Christian life, we'll constantly struggle to find an equilibrium between loving people and meeting their needs and loving ourselves and meeting our needs. But the Christian character trait of love means we choose not only to look after our own needs but also to escape the trap of self and to act compassionately toward others.

As we continue the process of training ourselves in love, love gets deeper down into our character. The acts of love that were so foreign become less so. We act in love more easily, and love finds its way into the deep-down parts of our character. The Holy Spirit expresses more of his fruit in our lives, and that fruit becomes mature, pleasing, beneficial to others.

Jesus said in John 13:35, "By this all men will know that you are my disciples, if you love one another." And in the first century, that's exactly what happened. Even a non-Christian historian said of the Christians in that era, "Behold, how they love one another." The first-century Christians had developed the character trait of love deep down in their persons. We can do the same.

When we have God's inner compassion for others, then our behavior will flow from a heart of love. We'll have integrity, and we'll be the same on the outside as on the inside. Our behavior will match our attitude of love:

> This is how we know what love is: Jesus Christ laid down his life for us. And we ought to lay down our lives for our brothers. If anyone has material possessions and sees his brother in need but has no pity on him, how can the love of God be in him? Dear children, let us not love with words or tongue but with actions and in truth. (1 John 3:16-18)

Those verses hit me squarely between the eyes. If we see a person in need, have the means to meet that need, and do nothing, then John says the love of God is not in us. Because God is a God of love, his children should reflect that love through concrete actions of helping others. We should use whatever material possessions we have—time, money, skill, a car, a house—in a balanced way to meet both our own valid needs and the valid needs of others. When God lives within, Christians tend to do that naturally.

Love in Action

Over the years I've heard many glowing testimonies from people who have been shown love in action. For instance, Marci, a fellow church member, became the victim of a rape and had to testify in court. The trauma of publicly telling her story was made worse by the presence in court of the perpetrator, a family friend. But she got through that day in court because a friend from church had taken off the day from work to sit in court with her.

When Joe's compact truck broke down fifty miles from home, Glen took Saturday off to tow it back with his full-size truck. Then Tom and Sam repaired it so Joe could drive to work on Monday.

What do you call these two cases? Examples of the normal Christian life, the Christian character trait of love. But we can't have deep-seated consistency in loving behavior until God himself rebuilds our character with his love. When God and his love are at the core of our character, we treat people differently. We think differently about ourselves. Our relationship with God deepens.

As we cultivate the presence of the Holy Spirit in our lives, as we follow him every moment of our day, as we allow love to be the foundation for our new character in Christ, we will see some major changes in who we are. Love becomes part of our identity and is seen in our behavior.

Steps Toward Character Change

1. Why do you think the have-it-your-way marketing strategies work so well? How susceptible are you and your friends to them?
2. Philippians 2:21 says, "For everyone looks out for his own interests, not those of Jesus Christ." What recent examples have you seen of selfishness in someone you know? Where have you seen selfishness in yourself?
3. What does love mean to you? Is it
   • a feeling?
   • an inner valuing of another, a valuing that causes you to act in the best interests of the person?
   Explain your answer.
4. On a scale of 1 to 5, with 1 representing "I have no love" and 5 representing "I most often respond with love," where would you place yourself? Why?
5. Do you think outward behavior is tied to inner character? Explain your answer and try to support it with Scripture.
6. What was Jesus' secret for being the same on the inside as on the outside? How can we be more like him?
7. Read 1 Corinthians 13. Which description of love is the most difficult for you to express? Why?
8. Describe a time when
   • you went beyond yourself to do something loving for another
   • you looked out for your own interests
9. Do you love with words, with actions, or both (see 1 John 3:18)? Give an example.

10. What weeds most threaten to choke out love in your life? How can you begin pulling those weeds?
11. List three things God has done recently to show his love for you. In what ways can you allow his love to grow in your life?
12. Ask someone you trust to help you think of specific ways to carry out the Christian character trait of love to those around you.

CHAPTER 4
Smiling through the Tears

Joy

But the fruit of the Spirit is . . . joy.
— PAUL THE APOSTLE, in GALATIANS 5:22

George's first job as a landscape contractor was to remove a large oak stump from a farmer's field. He also was using dynamite for the first time. With the farmer watching, George tried to hide his nervousness by carefully calculating the size of the stump, the proper amount of dynamite, and where to place it.

Finally he and the farmer moved to the detonator behind his pickup truck. With a silent prayer, George plunged the detonator. The stump gracefully rose through the air and then crashed on the cab of the truck. George gazed in despair at the ruined cab, but the farmer was all admiration.

"Son, with a little more practice, those stumps will land in the bed of the truck every time!"

When we face adversity, do we look at the crushed cab and give in to despair, depression, and discouragement? Or do we see how close to the bed we came and express joy and optimism?

God wants to instill in us his own character trait of joy, which doesn't depend upon the situation. God *is* joy. For Christians, joy is a realistic optimism that believes God's presence within us exceeds any difficulties threatening to overwhelm us.

The Bible consistently contrasts joy with sorrow, grief, despair, and discouragement. Each are chosen responses to the afflictions of life. Either we're driven to despair by difficulties, or with God we transcend them.

Ironically, joy comes only as we realize the difficulty of life. Joy isn't the absence of affliction. Hardship is normal. Disappointment and discouragement come when our hopes aren't realized. When we have the attitude life should be fair, we get depressed when it isn't. If we believe it's our right to have a high-paying, satisfying job, if we believe those we love should treat us with full consideration, if we believe our government should truly have the interests of its people at heart, then we're targets for discouragement, and joy will be hard to find. Cultivating the presence of God is the only way to transcend tribulation. Then, without denying the pain, we can smile through the tears of life.

If we want joy to be planted deep down in our lives, we need to understand that joy doesn't come from ease.

OUR NATURAL TENDENCY:
DIFFICULTY BRINGS PAIN

In John 16:33 Jesus promised us that life wouldn't be easy: "I have told you these things, so that in me you may have peace. In this world *you will have trouble*. But take heart! I have overcome the world" (emphasis mine).

I'm sure you've heard sermons proclaiming the "I have overcome the world" part of that verse. But have you ever heard a sermon on Jesus' promise of the reality of tribulation?

The Bible promises that God's people will go through

hard times. Read Hebrews 11, the faith chapter, beginning with verse 35. "Faith's Hall of Fame" lists people whose faith in God brought on many difficulties. They were tortured, beaten, imprisoned, stoned, cut in two, and sent to wander the wilderness in rags.

We must realize that hard times are just part of living in a world filled with pain and trouble. Following God doesn't grant us a reprieve from pain. In fact, it sometimes brings us more pain.

In the following sections of this chapter, we'll go into great detail in establishing that difficulties are indeed part of life and that godly people experience various forms of pain as a result. Why spend so much time on this one area? Because many leaders today teach that we "create our own reality." They teach that if we speak prosperity, ease, and health, we will receive them. They teach that if we believe, life will be easy. Some teach that to be sick, to be depressed, to worry, are signs of weak faith.

When we expect only good things to come our way and the reality of life doesn't match up, disappointment with God often follows. We think God didn't do his part. But the Bible makes it clear that difficulties *are* part of life, that even Christians get depressed, and that joy doesn't come from an easy life but from something deeper.

Let's examine five scriptural areas of difficulty we all face, using David—the man after God's own heart—as an example. Then we'll look at three typical and unhealthy reactions to difficulties. Our goal is to learn how to deal with these problems of life through the character trait of joy.

Five Areas of Difficulty
God wanted to bless David, a man after God's own heart. But did God remove difficulty from David's life to increase

his joy? Not at all. David experienced great suffering. Each adversity David faced represents an area we struggle in.

Physical Difficulties. Listen to David's pain in Psalm 31:10: "My life is consumed by anguish and my years by groaning; my strength fails because of my affliction, and my bones grow weak."

David went through physical distress. Whether the source of our suffering is illness, an accident, or undealt-with guilt, physical suffering is common in life. I'm discovering it's much more common now that I am forty-seven than it was when I was twenty-three. Minor sprains take months to heal. Our bodies age and decay. That was reality for David, and it is reality for us.

Friction with People. Some wit, or half-wit, proclaimed, "I like life; it's people I hate." We all struggle with people, and David did too:

> Because of all my enemies, I am the utter contempt of my neighbors; I am a dread to my friends—those who see me on the street flee from me. I am forgotten by them as though I were dead; I have become like broken pottery. For I hear the slander of many; there is terror on every side; they conspire against me and plot to take my life. (Psalm 31:11-13)

Our imperfection causes grief to others. We're not always understanding, kind, and forgiving. They aren't either. Their imperfections cause grief for us. Science defines friction as two uneven surfaces that rub against one another, producing heat. That sounds like a normal relationship! Even the best relationships go through struggles, and not all relationships are the best.

Unconfessed Sin. When we fail to acknowledge our sin,

that failure itself brings complications that sometimes exceed the consequences of our original sin. That's what David found in Psalm 38:3-8:

> Because of your wrath there is no health in my body; my bones have no soundness because of my sin. My guilt has overwhelmed me like a burden too heavy to bear. My wounds fester and are loathsome because of my sinful folly. I am bowed down and brought very low; all day long I go about mourning. My back is filled with searing pain; there is no health in my body. I am feeble and utterly crushed; I groan in anguish of heart.

Sound familiar? Complications of unconfessed sin range from overwhelming guilt to depression to physical infirmity.

Economic Adversity. Jesus promised we would always have the poor, and that promise is becoming more true all the time. We're in one of the worst recessions since the Great Depression. During the summer of 1994, one-third of all homes in our valley went back to the bank or mortgage company. That trend is continuing.

Homelessness spirals. High-tech jobs widen the gap between the upper and lower economic classes. Many people are unemployed or underemployed. Many people living in poverty work full time, but their wages aren't enough to live on. Economic adversity isn't new, according to David in Psalm 40:17: "Yet I am poor and needy; may the Lord think of me. You are my help and my deliverer; O my God, do not delay."

At times David had tremendous wealth; at other times he was poor. David's psalms reveal his grief at the abuse of the poor, at the problems poverty brings.

Death. We all face death—either our own or the death of those we love. Our youthful years of invincibility fade into the realization we're not exempt. Friends and family are unfairly taken from us, and we struggle as David did in Psalm 6:5: "No one remembers you when he is dead. Who praises you from the grave?" Considering death, we wonder at life's fairness, its meaning. And we don't want to relax our grip on life.

These problems are normal—normal in the sense that we should expect them and that we shouldn't be surprised when they happen. David, a man after God's own heart, wasn't protected from the presence of problems. We won't be either.

But how did David respond to them? Was David always happy and cheerful, like a superman? Or did these problems eat at him, attacking his faith in God? Did he question the fairness of life? Examining David's response, we discover we have much in common with this man.

Unhealthy Reactions to Difficulties

Being a typical human, David suffered with his struggles. Life's burdens weren't easy for him. Let's look at three of his unhealthy responses to difficulty.

Anxiety. All of us worry about how difficulties will impact our future. That's what David went through in Psalm 6:6: "I am worn out from groaning; all night long I flood my bed with weeping and drench my couch with tears."

Have you ever spent the night tossing and turning in bed, your mind going 100 m.p.h., chewing on a problem? All you sense is fear, the unknown, and loss. I've spent more than one sleepless night over a problem in the church, a personal issue, or the difficulties of a friend. Concern and worry seem to possess us. We feel helpless, out of control.

We feel responsible for the situation, and anxiety multiplies our pain.

Physical Problems. We're created with three parts: soul, spirit, and body. But we're one person; what affects one part will affect the other parts. Some doctors say up to 75 percent of all illness originates in our mind.

Many people react to stress with physical illness. David experienced that in Psalm 6:7: "My eyes grow weak with sorrow; they fail because of all my foes." We become listless and get the flu and colds with greater frequency and regularity. Why? Because our bodies are linked to our minds and emotions.

Depression. "Be merciful to me, O Lord," David prayed, "for I am in distress; my eyes grow weak with sorrow, my soul and my body with grief. My life is consumed by anguish and my years by groaning; my strength fails because of my affliction, and my bones grow weak" (Psalm 31:9-10).

When we feel overpowered by a difficulty, depression often results. We can't find energy to do anything. Emotionally, we want to give up. Despair takes over. Sorrow is a close friend, but not a good one. When we see the proverbial light at the end of the tunnel, we know it's just an onrushing train.

A non-Christian in this condition must have penned the phrase, "Life is tough. Then, you die." It's easy to look at life through gray-colored glasses. We expect the worst and receive it. Our shoulders droop. Our voices lower. Our eyes look down. A frown perpetually covers our face.

All we see is the crushed cab, the huge bill to repair it, the days we won't have the truck for work, and the laughingstock we'll be to the community.

Initial responses of anxiety, sickness, and depression are

typical, for David and for us. But we shouldn't feel guilty about them, as if we're spiritual failures. But our long-term response comes from how our character interacts with our perception of life. Is life our friend or our foe? And most important, what makes life good or bad? This is where the Christian character trait of optimism, or joy, comes in.

THE CHRISTIAN CHARACTER TRAIT OF JOY

We frequently confuse happiness and joy. Webster does, basically calling joy the emotion we have when things go our way. But the Christian character trait of joy comes from the center of our being and is independent of life's difficulties. A joyful character produces an optimistic outlook on life, so we'll use the terms *joy* and *optimism* interchangeably.

Joy Defined

Joy doesn't come from external circumstances. But happiness does. *Happiness* results from what's *happening*. Typically, when good things happen, we're happy. When bad things happen, we're not happy.

A sugar package found in a restaurant said, "An optimist is someone who tells you to cheer up, when things are going his way." Well, that's not optimism; that's happiness. The difference is major. If our *optimism* comes from external circumstances, we'll be up when things go as we desire, and we'll be down when they don't go as we desire. Even great spiritual victories won't bring lasting joy.

After Elijah's tremendous victory over the prophets of Baal, he was filled with fear and depression (see 1 Kings 18–19). Anxious about the consequences for his life, he was ready to die. Why? His focus was on the externals, not on the inward presence of God. Only that inward presence produces optimism.

God offers us a change of character so that we can consistently have joy in our life, regardless of the difficulties. As John Sanderson says in his book *The Fruit of the Spirit*, "Joy does not depend on outer circumstances, but on the reality of God."

Let me share my working definition of joy: Joy is "believing the reasons to be excited about life are greater than the reasons to get discouraged and negative."

Godly joy enables us to not merely react as a puppet, with our emotions moving up or down. Optimism allows us to *choose* our response. We may not always be happy, but we can always be optimistic. As we analyze the source of joy, we'll see the truth of that.

The Source of Joy

If happiness comes from what's happening, then joy and enthusiasm come from deep down. We'll look at two specific sources of joy: the presence of God within the deepest recesses of our life and God's work for our good in trials.

Joy through the Presence of God. Many verses link joy and the presence of God in our lives (see Acts 16:34; Romans 14:17; 1 Thessalonians 1:6). For now, let's just look at Psalm 16:8-11:

> I have set the Lord always before me. Because he is at my right hand, I will not be shaken. Therefore my heart is glad and my tongue rejoices; my body also will rest secure, because you will not abandon me to the grave, nor will you let your Holy One see decay. You have made known to me the path of life; *you will fill me with joy in your presence,* with eternal pleasures at your right hand. (emphasis mine)

Look at that last sentence. We gain the Christian character trait of joy from the presence of God. His presence proves that the reasons to be excited about life are greater than the reasons to become discouraged and negative.

Real reasons to get discouraged exist, as David experienced. But problems aren't all of the story. A Christian living in perpetual gloom is somewhat like reading a murder mystery only to the point where the murder occurs and then putting the book down, discouraged that the murder hasn't been solved. But it's not over. We haven't read the end.

Yes, Jesus did say that we'll have trouble in this world (John 16:33). Sometimes we whimper a weak amen at that verse, but we quit reading too soon. Jesus finished by saying, "But take heart! I have overcome the world." The same Jesus who overcame the world lives in us. We don't have to get dragged down by negativity. We don't have to retreat to a rose-colored-glasses view of reality, ignoring pain. We counter real problems with the overcoming presence of God in our hearts.

We need to grab on to the principle that the awesomeness of God's presence more than overbalances the tendency to get discouraged. The majestic, transcendent Creator of everything lives within us! When we continually repeat that thought until it becomes a habit, joy gets deep down. That trait establishes our outlook on life as optimistic, positive, and enthusiastic.

If we can't get excited about the concept of God living within us, then we get excited about the wrong things. If God's presence isn't enough to overcome any problem, then we have much too small a view of God.

When looking at problems heightens our negativity, we need to balance that by thinking about the God who lives within. And that's enthusiasm. *Enthusiasm* comes from a compound Greek word: *En,* meaning "in," and *theos,* meaning "God." We have enthusiasm when we realize we are *in God.*

Enthusiasm doesn't exist because the circumstances of life go well. Much of the time things don't go well. But optimism grows within us as a character trait when we're convinced that God is in us. To paraphrase an old line, "God's in my life; all's right with the world." This is perspective. If we primarily focus on the bad in life, if we suspect the future will bring only more pain, then depression and discouragement are inescapable. Problems grow in both number and magnitude until they become overwhelming.

But if we primarily focus on God's presence, then the future holds little fear. Optimism and joy are normal responses. We neither ignore nor are overwhelmed with life's problems. With a high view of God's love and power, his presence becomes more important than the presence of problems. No circumstance can overshadow that.

Some problems may succeed at discouraging us for a short time. That temporary depression afflicted both David and Elijah. But depression doesn't have to become a permanent part of our life, not when the discouragements are balanced with the powerful and exuberant presence of the Creator.

We find joy through the presence of God in our life. And that's how we find joy in the worst of our troubles.

Joy in the Midst of Trials. Morrie came to Christ late in life. Raised as a Jew with an awareness of spiritual matters, that awareness rarely impacted how he lived. His ambition drove him to the vice presidency of a major corporation, with debris strewn along the way. In the debris were fractured relationships with his wife and children.

Shortly before Morrie's retirement, cancer and a bad heart threatened to end his life. But God used a gently persistent hospital chaplain and a midnight vision to bring him to Christ. Morrie left the hospital with the cancer removed, the heart repaired, and the Spirit of the Lord living in him.

Five years, combined with an inquiring, hungry heart, provided the impetus to relational healing and spiritual growth. Then the cancer returned to stay. In his home on October 31, Halloween, Morrie went home to be with the God he had come to know and love. A comment that day by his son, Nate, struck an ironic note: "I've always hated Halloween because it's Satan's day. But I'm going to look at Halloween differently now. My dad beat Satan at his own game, on his day."

Did Morrie's death bring sorrow? Obviously. His family and friends lost someone they loved. But God's presence added joy to the anguish.

Joy can be found in the worst of trials because God is always within. "Consider it pure joy, my brothers, whenever you face trials of many kinds, because you know that the testing of your faith develops perseverance. Perseverance must finish its work so that you may be mature and complete, not lacking anything" (James 1:2-4).

The principles in that verse go against our grain. Consider it *pure joy* when the storms of life come? Some joy, maybe. Pure joy, no way. Are we excited at trials because we're masochistic and love to feel pain? Not at all. We can experience joy because we know God will use pain to perfect us, to make us all we can be. How does that work?

When Michelangelo was asked how he created the masterpiece *David*, he responded, "I merely got a piece of marble and chiseled away anything that didn't look like David."

If the marble had a nervous system, I'm sure the pain level would have been high as parts of its being were pounded off. But look at the result.

Think back on the easy, good times, the kind of times we are happy about. Did that happiness cause us to dig deeply into the meaning of life, to ask just who we were? Did happiness cause us to refine ourselves to eliminate any impurities? Or did we just savor those times and float along downstream?

Think back also on some of the more difficult times. Didn't that pain build a desire to eliminate what caused the grief, to discover what in us had caused the situation? The trials of life force us to search, meditate, and change.

How do we grow into the mature Christian life? How does God implant joy in us? God gives us joy by helping us work through difficulties. We find joy when we discover what "doesn't look like David" in our persons and allow God to chisel that away. We find joy by developing endurance rather than quitting at the first sign of hardship. We find joy by being committed to the process of how God works in us. The crises of life motivate us to eliminate anything that shouldn't be there.

Joy doesn't come from being caught up in the present pain but from seeing the eventual result. Satan will attempt to use painful events to bring discouragement and depression. God will use those same events to bring maturity and completion. What will bring more joy than to accomplish the opposite of what Satan is trying to do?

We beat Satan at his own game when we turn events that normally bring pain into joy. When we look at the long-term effects rather than the short-term effects of pain, we can have the character trait of joy through difficulties. We can smile through the tears of life.

This connection of joy and problems confuses most non-Christians because all they can see is pain, loss, and no hope. While just in his thirties, Sam died unexpectedly of a heart attack, leaving behind a wife and several young children. The owner of the apartment building Sam managed was a member at our church, and he asked me to do the funeral service. Sam, his family, and his friends did not have any background of faith or church involvement. Although you can't "preach someone into heaven," I tried at the funeral to focus on reasons to celebrate the life of the person. I brought out Sam's good points and gave the people a chance to share precious memories. Despite that, gloom hung over the crowd like a dark cloud. People couldn't begin to smile through their tears because they didn't have the Presence who can transform trouble. They couldn't comprehend hope.

We Christians face the same dark clouds of life. We cry. We grieve. We get depressed and discouraged. We're tempted to give up. But difficulties don't defeat us. Pain doesn't put us down because we know the end of the story. We have hope. We can enjoy life even when it brings pain. Although some accuse Christians of "pretending," of ignoring reality, actually we know reality even more than they do. It is the reality of God working in the worst of times to bring the best, in time.

CULTIVATING JOY

As a fruit of the Spirit, joy develops over time. But we must take the step to eliminate qualities that work against joy. The most dangerous weed in our garden of joy is negativity: When we expect bad experiences to come, they will overcome us. Pessimism destroys optimism, unless we weed it out.

Weeding Out Negativity

Philippians 4:4 calls us to rejoice always. That joy grows into a character trait when we change our thought life: "Finally, brothers, whatever is true, whatever is noble, whatever is right, whatever is pure, whatever is lovely, whatever is admirable—if anything is excellent or praiseworthy—think about such things" (Philippians 4:8).

Is looking for the bad noble? Is focusing on our problems lovely? Is complaining about our situation praiseworthy? Godly joy comes from our thoughts about life. When our thoughts are filled with the problems, we don't have room to rejoice over the presence of God.

How do we drive out negative thoughts? If we tell ourselves, *Don't think negatively*, all we think of is the negative. But if we replace them with positive thoughts, we eliminate the negative thoughts that bring depression and discouragement. Positive thoughts are those that build on the presence of God in our lives and enhance joy in our deep-down character.

NURTURING THE FRUIT OF JOY

When Morrie's son, Nate, dealt with his grief over his father's death by realizing his dad had beaten Satan on his own day, he was eliminating destructive thoughts and finding a reason to rejoice.

In studying verses about joy, I was amazed by what I didn't find. Not a single verse told me how to rejoice; the verse said just to do it. How do we eliminate those poisonous, negative thoughts? By finding a reason to rejoice and rejoicing. Joy is a natural response when we remind ourselves of several truths we can always be optimistic about.

Focus on God's Presence

When we think of how the awesome God lives in us, we can get excited. As we think of what he's done to show his love for us, we can get enthusiastic. As we think of how in the worst of times God was there, hugging us closely, we can celebrate. We build joy into a deep-down trait as we train ourselves to focus on his presence.

When a new believer (who hadn't been taught that prayer is a certain time alone with God) read the verse, "Pray at all times," he pondered how to pray while driving, at work, and in conversations. Finally he decided to begin each day with "Dear God, . . ." and to end his day with "In Jesus' name, Amen." He learned what it means to live in the presence of God!

Remember Psalm 16:11: "You will fill me with joy in your presence"? That means that as we cultivate an awareness of God's continual presence with us, we cultivate the trait of joy. Why? Can you think of anything more exciting than always being with the Creator of the universe? Imagine the person you most admire. Wouldn't you be thrilled to spend several hours with him or her, asking any question you desired, learning from that person, or just quietly being with him or her?

For a Christian, nobody should excite us like God. Just being with God is far better than the worst situation is bad. As we build on that, we find a reason to rejoice despite the circumstances.

Remember Eventual Victory

Another step in nurturing joy is to remind ourselves of the victory God guarantees us in the worst problems. As stated earlier, Jesus made two promises in John 16:33: First, as long as we walk this earth, we'll have trouble; second, we can take heart because Jesus has overcome the world. But we need to be cautious. Jesus doesn't free us *from* problems; he takes us *through* them. He doesn't eliminate our problems; rather, he gives us the power to not get dragged down and be overwhelmed by them.

We also need to remember we claim the ultimate victory. Despite all of Satan's attempts to use circumstances to draw us away from God, we have the power to conquer Satan's grasp on death and reach heaven. This truth brought joy to Morrie's family at his death. Satan won a skirmish, but Morrie won the war.

An effective tool to nurture joy is remembering difficult situations where God brought victory. The choice is ours: to nurture memories of defeat or victory. If we see defeat, we experience discouragement. If we see victory, we experience joy. And our joy will grow as we nurture memories of victory.

Remind Ourselves of Growth Opportunities

Another step in nurturing joy is to remember how God works for our spiritual growth in the worst of times.

Most of us are familiar with Romans 8:28, the promise that God will work for good in all things. Evil abounds and touches the lives of Christians. A godly life certainly does not eliminate pain (our study of David, earlier in this chapter, is a good example). But in the midst of evil, God continues to work effectively for good (see also James 1:2-4).

When life goes well, we tend to enjoy it, thinking we have it made. So we don't change; we don't dig deeper. But trials shatter our complacency. Our old methods don't work, and character weaknesses are revealed. We change, even if it's only a last resort. We eliminate anything that works against us, and we grow closer to God. We become more grounded and stable.

The James 1 passage teaches a key formula for developing the character trait of joy. Trials come, and we rejoice because we don't see just the short-term pain but also the long-term gain. We think, *If God allows a trial this big, he must have some great changes in store for me!*

And we rejoice, not at the pain—after all, we're not masochists—but at the opportunity to make significant spiritual growth. It is then we can smile through the tears of life.

STEPS TOWARD CHARACTER CHANGE

1. How do you define joy? Is it based on circumstances or the presence of God in your life?
2. Do you think joy is a choice? Explain your response and support it with Scripture verses, if possible.
3. Describe a difficult time you've faced. In what ways did you see God work for victory and growth in that time?
4. On a scale of 1 to 5, with 1 representing "I have no joy" and 5 representing "I most often respond with joy," what number describes your level of joy? Explain.
5. What weeds threaten to choke out joy in your life? What can you do to pull these weeds?
6. At what times do you feel the closest to God? What activities enhance your sense of his presence in your life? Why?
7. What can you do to nurture joy? Be specific.
8. Share the specific decision you have made to nurture joy in your life with someone you trust. Ask him or her to hold you accountable to act on that decision in the months ahead.

CHAPTER 5

Slowing Our Spirit

Peace

But the fruit of the Spirit is . . . peace.
— PAUL THE APOSTLE, in GALATIANS 5:22

In the comic strip *Sally Forth*, Sally has just finished a pile of paperwork in the middle of a hectic day. Then she asks her secretary if any messages came in.

Marcie looks down at her desk. "Let's see, Ralph's looking for you. You've got twelve calls to return. Here's your mail. Your baby-sitter wants you to get back to her—right away. Your husband phoned, he's working late tonight . . . and you're ten minutes late for your two o'clock meeting."

Sally sighs. "The trouble with life in the fast lane is, there's no finish line."

The pace of life overwhelms us. We wait for things to slow down, and they merely increase their speed. We feel like a puppet dancing on the end of a string somebody else jerks around. We have more projects than time. We get intimidated by the pace of technology.

Worst of all, we can't slow life down and make it more manageable. At the end of a long day, a pastor turned to his secretary and said, "I just want a little quiet. Some peace. No rushing about."

She replied, "I understand. I believe they call that a funeral."

We probably won't slow the pace of life on this side of the

grave; too many factors are beyond our control. High housing costs force us to keep unpleasant jobs that pay well. Too many recreational and educational activities for our children drain our time. Job pressures force overtime. A complex culture conspires to suck up our time and energy. We can't easily change those forces.

But we can slow our spirit. We can nurture the Christian character trait of peace to bring a tranquility that transcends the tempo of our times. God wants to instill in us his own character trait of peace. But peace isn't inherent in us. We tend to go the opposite direction.

OUR NATURAL TENDENCY: WORRY

The biblical word for worry suggests having a divided mind, being torn in two directions. We want to find peace through trusting God, but we also feel we need to take responsibility, to do something. Worry is having two opposite concerns warring with one another. And when worry over the stresses of life consumes our thoughts, peace isn't an option.

We see all the things needed to be done, how little time we have, and we worry. According to Jesus, anxiety is the opposite of finding peace through trust in God:

> Therefore I tell you, do not worry about your life, what you will eat or drink; or about your body, what you will wear. Is not life more important than food, and the body more important than clothes? Look at the birds of the air; they do not sow or reap or store away in barns, and yet your heavenly Father feeds them. Are you not much more valuable than they? Who of you by worrying can add a single hour to his life? . . . So

do not worry, saying, "What shall we eat?" or "What shall we drink?" or "What shall wear?" For the pagans run after all these things, and your heavenly Father *knows that you need them*. But seek first his kingdom and his righteousness, and all these things will be given to you as well. Therefore do not worry about tomorrow, for tomorrow will worry about itself. Each day has enough trouble of its own. (Matthew 6:25-27, 31-34, emphasis mine)

Those issues of food, clothing, and shelter drive us to worry and steal our peace. If we focus on getting and holding on to them, anxiety consumes us. We have too much to do, too little time, too few resources. The alternative to being stressed over the stuff and pace of life is the Christian character trait of peace or tranquility. The ability to slow our spirit in the rush of life.

THE CHRISTIAN CHARACTER TRAIT OF PEACE

Peace isn't the absence of difficulty, stress, and being rushed. The character trait of tranquility allows us to relax in the midst of a bustling society. Although we can't stop the world from making frantic demands on our time, energy, and activities, we can still find peace.

Peace Defined

An art competition awarded a prize for the best expression of peace. One painting depicted a deer and fawn grazing at the skirt of a mountain meadow rimmed with pines and cedars stretching heavenward. Another showed a cat curled up in a basket, resting with all its being, as only cats can do.

But first prize went to the painting of a tumultuous

waterfall. Torrents rushed downward to dash themselves on the rocks below, sending spray high above. A tree branch extended just above the mist, with a bird's nest in a fork. Safely within was the mother bird and two babies.

That's tranquility. The ability to relax in the most rushed circumstances. Serene surroundings don't produce peace. The absence of animosity doesn't. If peace depended on the setting, many could never find serenity.

Peace is being in harmony, allowing God to fit all the pieces of our lives together. As we cultivate the presence of the Holy Spirit deep down, he brings peace.

Personal Peace

Peace begins on the personal level, between an individual and God. Personal peace comes when Jesus Christ is the passion that drives our lives. Lacking that kind of passion will bring unrest and dissatisfaction. In the first page of his *Confessions*, Augustine wrote, "Thou has made us for Thyself, and our heart is restless until it finds rest in Thee."

The psychologist Carl Jung echoed our central need for God: "Among all my patients in the second half of life, that is to say, over 35, there has not been one whose problem in the last resort was not that of finding a religious outlook on life."

Peace comes only from God. A variety of problems result when God isn't at the center of our lives. The only source of secure peace is intimately knowing God: "Therefore, since we have been justified through faith, we have peace with God through our Lord Jesus Christ" (Romans 5:1).

On my Honda Gold Wing motorcycle, power comes to the rear wheel through the hub. The hub at the center of the wheel receives the power and transmits it through the spokes to the rim. The wheel then moves. Think of our lives as that wheel. The hub is the center of our lives, what motivates and drives us. The spokes are the specific areas, like our personality, character, activities. The rim is the outer part of our lives that shows action. If our spokes aren't firmly connected to God at the hub of our lives, we won't move.

We may have action. The hub moves; the spokes may even flop around. But the rim doesn't move. Despite the activity, little is accomplished. However, when all the pieces of our lives are connected to God, we can have peace and harmony. Our lives may never slow down; we may not be able to escape the pace of life. But we can unify everything under Christ.

We're not torn in two directions, or even twenty, all at the same time. We go in one direction with God. We evaluate all activities out of a desire to please him. Like the bird's nest above the waterfall, we rest easy during the storms of life.

Anxiety over paying the mortgage doesn't possess our thoughts. We trust in God's promise to meet our needs when we put him first. We're not in constant fear over health issues. Either we die, which brings us directly to the love of our life; or we live and serve God here on earth. If our health improves, we're pleased; but if it doesn't we know that God's power is made perfect in our weakness (2 Corinthians 12:9). Concern over government officials and school boards doesn't bring depression: which person can oppose what God truly wants done?

Instead of worrying or feeling rushed, we focus on pleasing him. By relying on God as the center of our lives, all the pieces of our existence connect. We have completeness. We have peace. We trust in God's love and power and yield personal responsibility for how things develop.

Interpersonal Peace

Once we have personal peace with God, then we can develop peace with others. This doesn't mean we bring in world peace and abolish war, but that God brings peace between those he lives within. The apostle Paul commands us to have peace within the church: "Finally, brothers, good-by. Aim for perfection, listen to my appeal, be of one mind, *live in peace*. And the *God of* love and *peace* will be with you" (2 Corinthians 13:11, emphasis mine).

Solving world violence exceeds both our grasp and our responsibility. Slowing down the hectic pace that drives us is likewise impossible. But within the church we can live in peace. How? By being "of one mind." When our minds are passionately united on the shared importance of God, any differences we have are secondary. Yes, we disagree on when and how Jesus is coming. Yes, we disagree on spiritual gifts. Yes, we disagree on almost anything. But our shared passion for Jesus Christ exceeds our differences. That passion bonds us together in peace.

Too often, peace in the local church is merely something we read about. We've all seen or experienced examples of this all-deserved description: "The church is the only army that shoots its wounded." I know of two churches that split over the color of carpeting in the fellowship hall—a direct result of placing personal preference above peace.

When I was growing up, my church's slogan set the stage for peace: "On essential matters of faith, we have unity; on nonessential matters of opinion, we have liberty; but in all things, we have love." Have we lived up to this consistently? Not as much as God would desire. But it's a goal that allows us to have peace.

If we insist on our opinions, we'll battle and never have peace in our churches. But if we can unite around our shared passion for Christ, lesser issues slip into the background. Peace reigns between brothers and sisters.

By aiming for perfection, with a common mind-set that Jesus is most important, by yielding on our opinions for the mission of Christ, we can then obey Paul's command to live in peace.

CULTIVATING PEACE

Ron's job of supervising computer programmers requires driving two and a half hours each way, into the thick of southern California traffic. Crawling along at 5 m.p.h. when you're late for work doesn't build tranquility. Nor does returning to a houseful of three outgoing, noisy teenagers. Add to this, serving as an elder in your church and heading a calling-on-visitors program, and you wouldn't guess this to be a recipe for tranquility.

But Ron is one of the most peaceful, gracious men I know. Troubles tend to bring a smile, unruly children provoke firm but loving discipline with no angry outbursts. People are drawn to his serenity. How does he do it? Ron learned that developing tranquility first requires eliminating weeds that compete with the fruit of peace.

Weeding Out Worry, Friction, and Artificial Fruit

Just as a vegetable garden needs to be weeded to eliminate plants that compete with the desired result, we need to eliminate traits in our lives that work against peace.

Worry. According to Philippians 4:6-7, the first weed to pluck out is worry: "Do not be anxious about anything, but in everything, by prayer and petition, with thanksgiving, present your requests to God. And the *peace of God*, which transcends all understanding, will guard your hearts and your minds in Christ Jesus" (emphasis mine).

We achieve peace by eliminating worry, that preoccupation with our responsibility to work out things in our lives. Prayer is the antidote to worry. Peace develops when we pray and invite God to direct our lives. We don't become irresponsible. We still do our part, but we give the responsibility for results to God. That's what prayer is all about. The more we pray, the more peace we possess.

Friction with People. We can't ensure great relationships with everyone, but we can do our part to get along well with people. The traits listed in Galatians 5:19-21 work against the fruit of peace: "The acts of the sinful nature are obvious: sexual immorality, impurity and debauchery; idolatry and witchcraft; hatred, discord, jealousy, fits of rage, selfish ambition, dissensions, factions and envy; drunkenness, orgies, and the like." Those acts involve other people—using them for our own purposes. To the degree we allow qualities like dissension and envy, we decrease our tranquility. To the degree we work against these qualities, we increase peace.

Artificial Fruit. We also need to be on guard against the counterfeit fruit of apathy. Some lead very tranquil, peaceful lives. They feel no stress; they're relaxed. Why? They just don't care; they possess no passion. Whatever happens is OK. Ephesians 4:19 talks of people who have "lost all sensitivity," who are past feeling.

But that's not peace. Peace isn't giving up on the battles of life, but continuing to fight the good fight with harmony and contentment. Peace isn't the absence of passion, nor the absence of struggle. Peace has a passion that unites a person's life in the struggles. So don't allow apathy to masquerade as peace in your life. Instead, cultivate the Christian character trait of tranquility.

NURTURING THE FRUIT OF PEACE

How do we nurture peace in our lives? We build tranquility into a deep-seated character trait in three steps.

Step One: Develop a Conscious Trust in God

First, we deepen our relationship with God. Listen to the promise in Isaiah 26:3: "You will keep *in perfect peace* him whose mind is steadfast, because he *trusts in you*" (emphasis mine).

When we keep our minds firmly on the love and grace of God and trust in his provision for us, then we can rest in his peace. But if we don't keep our minds solidly on God, if we allow the demands of contemporary life to overwhelm us, we feel like a marionette—dancing every time somebody pulls our string.

The more we nurture continual contact with almighty God, the more peace imbeds itself in our character.

Step Two: Pray

One method of nurturing contact with God is to pray at all times, for all things: "Don't worry about anything; instead, pray about everything. . . . If you do this, you will experience God's peace, which is far more wonderful than the human mind can understand" (Philippians 4:6-7, TLB). The key to peace is prayer. And continual prayer is living in the presence of God. We may not talk, but we know he's there. We may not consciously listen, but we sense his presence.

Peace comes through exhaustive prayer, when nothing is too big or too small to take to God. When we think an issue is small enough to be our sole responsibility, we build anxiety. When we think an issue exceeds even God's ability to overcome, we eliminate the only solution to worry. But as we pray at all times for all things we can rest easy in God's ability to take care of us.

Step Three: Commit to the Local Church

The next step in promoting the trait of tranquility deals with our connection to fellow Christians. In Ephesians 4:3, Paul tells the church how to be the church and that unity and peace are essential elements: "Make every effort to *keep the unity of the Spirit* through the *bond of peace*" (emphasis mine).

The church isn't always peaceful. We're known for major fights over minor items. But that violates the blueprint God gives for his church. We cannot have peace, either personally or interpersonally, until we're committed to and in harmony with the local church. We won't always agree with other members or the leadership. No church will fully meet our needs and desires. As long as people are in them, local churches will be imperfect.

But Christians are still called to be part of the church. The Christian who won't commit to a local church is somewhat like a firefighter who won't go to the station, who won't fight fires with the other firefighters but still strongly professes he "believes in fighting fires."

Harmony provides a combined power exceeding what we can accomplish as individuals. In a horse-pulling contest in Canada, the winning horse pulled nine thousand pounds. The next finisher moved eight thousand pounds. Then the owners harnessed the two horses, expecting them to pull about seventeen thousand pounds. Instead, working together in harmony, they moved thirty thousand pounds.

What have we not accomplished for God because we won't work together in peace? What price have we paid for our independence? Is it possible Christ would have returned centuries ago if the church had just worked together in peace?

God's solution for the fast pace of life is the Christian

character trait of peace: an inner tranquility that transcends the situation, an ability to slow our spirit in the midst of more demands than we can respond to. Peace puts God at the hub of our lives, allowing him to organize the details, to be responsible for the outcome. As we develop a passion for God, valuing him above all else and trusting him, peace grows deep in our inner character.

STEPS TOWARD CHARACTER CHANGE

1. Do you ever feel rushed and overwhelmed? At what times and in what areas?
2. What have you done to try to change that overwhelmed feeling? How effective were you?
3. How do you define *peace?*
4. On a scale of 1 to 5, with 1 representing "I have no peace" and 5 representing "I most often respond with peace," what number would you choose for yourself? Why?
5. If you asked other church members, your family, or friends, do you think they would say you are a source of peace or irritation? Why? If you are an irritation, how can you remedy that?
6. What weeds most threaten to choke out joy in your life? How can you begin to pull those weeds?
7. Do you think prayer is an antidote to worry? Why or why not? How does prayer work for you?
8. How much of a passion do you have for God? What can you do in the upcoming weeks to build tranquility in your life?
9. Share with a trusted friend one or two steps you plan to take to allow peace to grow in your life. Ask him or her to hold you accountable, particularly during the stressful times.

CHAPTER 6

Hanging in There

Patience

But the fruit of the Spirit is . . . patience.
—PAUL THE APOSTLE, in GALATIANS 5:22

While piloting a commuter flight from Portland, Maine, to Boston, Henry Dempsey heard a strange noise coming from the rear of the small plane. Turning the controls over to his copilot, he went to check it out. Just as he discovered the rear door hadn't been secured before takeoff, the plane hit an air pocket, slamming Henry against the door. The door flew open; Henry was sucked out of the open doorway toward the ocean below.

The copilot saw the open door warning light and realized Henry had disappeared. He radioed in, requesting a helicopter search for that area of the ocean.

After the plane landed, they found Henry. But he wasn't floating in the ocean beneath the flight path. Almost miraculously, he had grabbed onto the outside ladder and held on as the plane descended from four thousand feet at 200 m.p.h. During the landing, he kept his head above the runway, only twelve inches away. Dempsey's fingers had to be pried from the ladder.

That's called "hanging in there." We all face turbulence in life and come to the point where we *don't* want to hang in there. For example, our boss makes unreasonable demands on us, so we start reading the help-wanted ads. Someone in church offends us by a chance comment, and we're ready to start looking. Again. Our mate treats us like last week's leftovers, and we wonder how a divorce would affect the kids. A jerk darts in front of us on the freeway so we have to slam on our brakes, and we are ready to quit being Mr. Nice Guy. We've reached the end of our rope, and we want to use it to strangle the next person who tells us to tie a knot in it and hang on.

This is where our Christian character comes into play. The trait of patience gives us the desire and ability to "hang in there." As a pastor who counsels people in the worst of times, I sometimes find that nothing helps more than the simple encouragement of that phrase.

As a fruit of the Spirit, patience enables us to not be overwhelmed by despair and to control our anger when offended. We don't typically respond that way.

OUR NATURAL TENDENCY: ANGER
OR DISCOURAGEMENT

When dealing with problem situations, our typical responses are either with anger or the desire to give up.

Anger

According to Proverbs 14:29, patience is the opposite of anger: "A patient man has great understanding, but a quick-tempered man displays folly." When offended, our anger can rise up out of control. We want to give our enemies what they deserve—and maybe just a little more to encourage them to never do it again. But that is foolish. Usually we make the situation worse, and we burn the bridges of reconciliation.

Discouragement

When injustice rules, when our money is meager, when

failures mount, we often feel like giving up. The high suicide rate among our population expresses this, as does Psalm 37:7: "Be still before the Lord and wait patiently for him; do not fret when men succeed in their ways, when they carry out their wicked schemes." The opposite of patience is fretting. We lose heart and get depressed. We get emotionally overwrought. We become tired of always having to strive and fight, only to receive so little.

When we respond in anger or discouragement, we're wishing the problems of life would disappear. But we can't change the outside world we live in, merely our inner character.

THE CHRISTIAN CHARACTER
TRAIT OF PATIENCE

God gives us the ability to respond to life's problems with patience, which is a part of the character he imbeds within us. Patience allows us to face trials without anger or discouragement.

Patience Defined

This may not sound like good news, but the literal meaning of patience is "long suffering": to be able to continue to suffer from the unfairness of life and not quit. Or, to hang in there.

Patience has two basic expressions. First, that we use self-restraint in the face of provocation and do not retaliate instantly. This focuses on our anger, on patience as the opposite of being quick-tempered. We may have a valid reason to retaliate, but we don't. Second, patience means we don't surrender to circumstances. We don't quit when life gets difficult. We don't give in to despair. This is the opposite of despondency, when we think there's no way out.

83

For most of us, patience isn't a natural or easy response. The only way we can consistently express patience is to realize the source is God, not ourselves.

God's Patience

When we allow the God who lives in us to implant his character in us, God's patience becomes a part of us. Patience defines who God is, according to 1 Timothy 1:16: "But for that very reason I was shown mercy so that in me, the worst of sinners, Christ Jesus might display *his unlimited patience* as an example for those who would believe on him and receive eternal life" (emphasis mine).

God restrains himself when we ought to be Post Toasties. God doesn't give up on us, no matter how we disappoint and fail him. Why? Because that's his character, and it's the pattern for us. God offers that same patience to each of us, but it takes work to make it part of our character.

CULTIVATING PATIENCE

To incorporate patience into our character, we first need to consciously eliminate qualities that work against patience.

Weeding Out Revenge and Doubts

We can have very good reasons to blast people or to get discouraged and quit. When we dwell on those valid reasons, patience will not develop. To get the fruit of patience growing in the garden of our lives, we need to weed out two qualities: our desire to get back at people and our doubts about God.

Personal Revenge. How do we nurture healthy relationships? Romans 12:9-21 tells us; and in the last three verses we find a key element: the injunction to not take revenge.

Do not take revenge, my friends, but leave room for God's wrath, for it is written: "It is mine to avenge; I will repay," says the Lord. On the contrary: "If your enemy is hungry, feed him; if he is thirsty, give him something to drink. In doing this, you will heap burning coals on his head." Do not be overcome by evil, but overcome evil with good.

God knows the hearts of people, their motives, their life situations. How many times have we been quick to respond in anger, only to later learn why a person's behavior was understandable?

As a working single mother, Sundays were important to Peggy. Contact with God refreshed her spirit; contact with others brought support and encouragement. But the hassles of getting a slow-moving teenage daughter ready on time took a toll on patience.

Already running late, Peggy got stuck on the freeway behind an elderly couple going well below the speed limit. Frustration built at being late to church. "Why do people so old even get on the freeway? Why can't they speed up? They're making me late to church!" she yelled.

Finally an opening in the next lane allowed her to slip in and pass the older couple. She looked over as she passed, ready to wither them with an angry glare, and discovered it was her beloved pastor and his wife.

Only God can balance justice and grace and not get carried away with emotions. Child abuse most often takes place when an adult overreacts in the white heat of anger, and discipline crosses over the line to abuse.

When God's character changes ours, we must yield the desire for our personal revenge and leave the situation up to God.

Doubts about God. Sometimes our frustration and discouragement comes from wondering if God really is in control of life: *If God truly loved me, would he give me this job just to take it away? If God's in charge of everything, why did I lose my house . . . or my car . . . or my mate? Why did my child die at such a young age?*

Discouragement comes when we doubt God's control. We see no light at the end of the tunnel. We're not convinced God will work all things out for good. Those doubts destroy patience. Frustration often occurs when we're not convinced God will do the right thing, or even anything. Psalm 40:1 has the solution: "I *waited patiently* for the Lord; he turned to me and heard my cry" (emphasis mine).

What is required for God to hear and respond? Patient waiting; suffering in the circumstances until the time is right for God to step in. When we weed out doubts that God will act, in his best time, we provide the environment for patience to grow.

NURTURING THE FRUIT OF PATIENCE
There are three key steps in incorporating the patience of God into our character: focusing on God's presence in our lives, relying on his sovereignty, and developing an attitude of perseverance.

Focus on God's Presence
In order to incorporate the fruit of patience into our character we must first practice the presence of God: "Be still before the Lord and wait patiently for him; do not fret when men succeed in their ways, when they carry out their wicked schemes" (Psalm 37:7). The last part of the verse gives our goal: to not fret at the injustice of life. The first part provides the method: to be still before God and to wait,

reminding ourselves that God is always with us. When our thoughts continually focus on the presence of God, worries and anger don't seem as oppressive.

This is the secret of the victorious Christian life: Remember that the all-conquering King lives within us and that he works in all things for good.

Alton Cooper was a big, tough, career marine. Everyone sensed it. But inside that gruff exterior lived a softhearted man who deeply loved God. While I was his pastor, exposure to Agent Orange in Vietnam caught up to him. Doctors first thought his testicular cancer could be treated and gave him a good prognosis for recovery. But the cancer spread to the prostate, then to the bones. And with the cancer came the pain.

That pain ravaged his once-strong body, but it never touched his spirit. Everyone in the hospital knew Alton loved his Lord. Daily he made his rounds, visiting other patients with a word of encouragement or expressing thanks to the hospital workers. On my frequent 130-mile round trips Alton ministered to me. Despite the pain, Alton had a peace through the suffering.

Finally, one of the doctors asked the question, "Mr. Cooper, we know the pain you're in. We know the suffering you're going through. But we don't know how you have this serenity. What's your secret?"

That was all the opening Alton needed. He shared how his trust in God didn't depend on life going his way, that God had always been there for him. Then he gave that doctor a copy of this poem by an unknown author. For me, it will always be "Alton's Poem."

I met God in the morning
When my day was at its best

And his presence came like sunrise
Like a glory in my breast.

All day long his presence lingered
All day long he stayed with me
And we sailed with perfect calmness
O'er a very troubled sea.

Other ships were blown and battered
Other ships were sore distressed
But the winds that seemed to drive them
Brought to us a peace and rest.

Then I thought of other mornings
With a keen remorse of mind
When I too had loosed the moorings
With the presence left behind.

So I think I know the secret
Learned from many a troubled day
You must seek God in the morning
If you want him through the day.

As your eyes open in the morning, as the fog of sleep drifts away, think of God. As you head for work, spend time alone with God, rather than planning your day. As you reach daily crossroads, times of decision, choose what he would have you do. Spend each moment in conscious contact with him.

When you spend time with God, being angry becomes more difficult; giving up becomes less desirable. What circumstance of life is as bad as God is good? Cultivating the presence of God enables us to be long-suffering.

Focus on God's Sovereignty

We also need to develop our awareness of God's power. Often our anger and frustration grow from a belief that life is out of control. Patience develops when we understand deep down that God *does* control life. Although our limited vision won't show us that control, God works to carry out his plan—and nothing can stop him.

Not all that happens matches what God desires. When people die without having given their lives to him, God's will is violated: "The Lord is not slow in keeping his promise, as some understand slowness. He is patient with you, *not wanting anyone to perish*, but everyone to come to repentance" (2 Peter 3:9, emphasis mine).

Yet, despite all the evil in the world, God will accomplish everything he has promised. He is sovereign.

Job learned that. If you don't know the story, read the book of Job to see how he faced difficulties that would destroy most of us. At times he thought God had abandoned him. But Job hung in there, and he learned a vital lesson: "I know that you can do all things; no plan of yours can be thwarted" (Job 42:2).

God's plan is to work for good in the lives of each believer, according to Romans 8:28: "And we *know* that in all things *God works for the good* of those who love him, who have been called according to his purpose" (emphasis mine).

When we have that deep-seated conviction that God will bring good out of the worst situation, we can have patience. We can avoid vengeance, knowing God will do something better. We can avoid quitting, knowing God still works for good. We can avoid despair and discouragement, knowing someday, somehow, good will come.

Trusting in God's sovereignty allows us to have patience,

to look beyond the tyranny of the now, where difficulties buffet us, to the long term, where the plan of God is accomplished.

Develop a Hang-in-There Attitude

To incorporate the patience of God we also need to have perseverance. In Hebrews 12:1-3, God gives us the option to hang in there regardless of the difficulty:

> Therefore, since we are surrounded by such a great cloud of witnesses, let us throw off everything that hinders and the sin that so easily entangles, and let us run *with perseverance* the race marked out for us. Let us fix our eyes on Jesus, the author and perfecter of our faith, who *for the joy set before him* endured the cross, scorning its shame, and sat down at the right hand of the throne of God. Consider him who *endured* such opposition from sinful men, *so that you will not grow weary and lose heart.* (emphasis mine)

Our race isn't a quick and easy hundred-yard dash, but a grueling, painful marathon. We must understand that the good times of life occur far less often than the depths. To see the awe-inspiring view, we must climb the mountain. And we mustn't quit.

On a Wisconsin dairy farm, two frogs fell into a bucket of cream and couldn't escape. One croaked, "Might as well give up. This stuff is too thick to swim in and too thin to jump. We're bound to die, so it might as well be now." He sank to the bottom and died. His friend just kept paddling, keeping afloat. By morning he was perched on the mound of butter he had churned, eating the flies drawn to the butter.

He hung in there. He didn't quit. And pardon the pun, but he came out on top. If a dumb frog knows enough not to quit, shouldn't we, with the Holy Spirit within, not give in to despair and anger?

Our power alone won't overcome the difficult situations we face. But Christians hang in there. We don't stay discouraged. We don't take revenge. We're in for the long haul. Why? Because God lives within us, and he gives us his own character trait of patience.

STEPS TOWARD CHARACTER CHANGE

1. Have you ever wanted to just crawl into a hole and hide? If so, what did you do in that situation? If you stayed out of the hole, what kept you out?
2. In what ways do you believe God is sovereign? (Try to support your answer from Scripture.)
3. How can those beliefs help you "hang in there" in difficult times?
4. What makes you angry? Do you think your anger usually is caused by the situation, or is it your choice to react that way? Explain.
5. How would you define *patience?*
6. On a scale of 1 to 5, with 1 representing "I have no patience" and 5 representing "I most often respond with patience," what number would you choose? Why?
7. What weeds most threaten to choke out patience in your life? How can you begin pulling those weeds?
8. Has there ever been a time when you wanted to get back at someone who wronged you, but you didn't? If so, how can you use that situation as a pattern for developing the fruit of patience in your life?

9. Describe a time when God showed his patience to you. How did that make you feel?
10. Decide on one active step you can take this week to further the growth of patience in your life. Then share it with someone you trust, and ask that person to pray with and for you as you take that step.

CHAPTER 7

Kind to the Bone

Kindness

But the fruit of the Spirit is . . . kindness.
—PAUL THE APOSTLE, in GALATIANS 5:22

Her beauty enabled her to manipulate men, and she did so with artistry. His leadership skills placed him in the position of guiding the nation, but he matched that with a weakness for ladies. They made a perfect match. Her attractiveness became so well known that, centuries later, underwear commercials featured her. His legendary strength made his name the standard for strong men. She discovered combining kindness with her beauty turned men into putty, and she gave just enough of herself to dig her hooks in deep. Their names? Samson and Delilah. Their story is in Judges 16.

But Delilah's kindness had a dark side. Unknown to Samson, she sold him out to his enemies. If she could discover the secret of his great strength, fifty-five hundred shekels of silver would change hands. She wined and dined him and finally wrenched the secret out of him. Because he couldn't resist her beauty and kindness, she ended up with the money, and he ended up with death. Delilah's kindness led to Samson's demise.

OUR NATURAL TENDENCY:
ARTIFICIAL KINDNESS

Before we get too righteously indignant at Delilah, do we share her trait? Do we also manipulate with kindness? Are we nice to people who can benefit us? Do we discount or ignore those who can't? When people treat us nicely, do we respond with niceness? And when others are rude and unforgiving, are we rude and unforgiving in return?

We've all known people who are "mean to the bone." They seem to live by the motto "If you can't say something good about a person, talk all you want." Their guiding principle is "Do unto others before they do unto you." A mean streak defines their character, and they delight in bringing grief to others.

Even as Christians we can recognize similar patterns. Whether we acknowledge a mean streak within us or merely recognize we use surface kindness to manipulate people, we miss being what God designed us to be.

God wants his people to be different. Rather than meanness, he desires we have kindness so deep within our character that we truly are "kind to the bone." We're designed by God to have kindness flow from our inner character to our outward behavior.

Although we may not currently be "mean to the bone," we need to be transformed by God living within so that kindness abounds. Human beings are a curious mixture of kindness and meanness. Sometimes we act with great altruism and sacrifice, and the next moment with petty selfishness. Both extremes represent true parts of who we are. But God desires something better for us: the consistent Christian character trait of kindness.

THE CHRISTIAN CHARACTER
TRAIT OF KINDNESS

When God's Spirit lives within us, he imbues us with God's character, including his trait of kindness. We have the opportunity to have kindness become not just a small part of our identity but a distinguishing feature.

Kindness Defined

The word listed in Galatians 5:22 for kindness translates into the English words *gentleness, goodness, excellence.* Kindness means we work well with people without being harsh, hard, sharp, or bitter. The word for kindness is often found next to the word for love. We can best understand the character trait of kindness as we examine scriptural examples of God's kindness.

God's Kindness

As I studied the Scriptures, I discovered God and kindness were usually linked together behaviorally. God *showed* his kindness. God's inner kindness expressed itself in what he did. Four intriguing aspects came out of my study.

God Is Kind to All. First, God's kindness reaches out to all, not just to some people. When we act as God does, we show we truly are his children. God acts in kindness without regard to our worthiness: "But love your enemies, do good to them, and lend to them without expecting to get anything back. Then your reward will be great, and you *will be* sons of the Most High, because *he is kind to the ungrateful and wicked*" (Luke 6:35, emphasis mine).

We show that we are children of God when we act like our Father, in kindness toward ungrateful enemies. Here we find the difference between *doing some kind things* and *being a kind person.* Everyone, even Delilah, does some kind

95

acts. We all can be kind toward the people we get along with, when being kind benefits us.

But kindness flows from our character when we consistently act in kindness toward those who don't deserve it. Does God show kindness only to people who deserve it? Of course not. None of us receives God's kindness on the basis of our own merit, but on the basis of God's character. God is kind. Therefore, he acts in kindness. The kindness isn't conditional upon the recipient but, the character of the giver.

God Blesses Us with Gifts of Nature. In kindness, God offers all people the benefits of the natural world. As Paul the apostle expressed to a group of unbelievers in the city of Lystra, God's kindness is not based on our merit: "He has *shown kindness* by giving you rain from heaven and crops in their seasons; he provides you with plenty of food and fills your hearts with joy" (Acts 14:17, emphasis mine).

God doesn't yield the blessings of nature just to godly people. Why? Because he's kind, and by nature he shows kindness to all.

God Offers Us Life in Christ. Titus 3:4-6 combines God's kindness, as an expression of his character, and our own unworthiness to have earned salvation: "But when the *kindness and love of God* our Savior appeared, he saved us, not because of righteous things we had done, *but because of his mercy.* He saved us through the washing of rebirth and renewal by the Holy Spirit, whom he poured out on us *generously* through Jesus Christ our Savior" (emphasis mine).

God sent his Son to die such a terrible death because his kindness saw the greater good. This same kindness causes him to act consistently in the best interests of mankind. But God's kindness has a condition: To receive the full measure of the kindness available to us, we need to persevere in our relationship with God.

God's Kindness Is Contingent on Our Perseverance. Romans 11:22 reveals two almost contrasting character traits of God, neither of which we dare ignore: "Consider therefore *the kindness and sternness of God*: sternness to those who fell, but kindness to you, *provided that you continue* in his kindness. Otherwise, you also will be cut off" (emphasis mine).

God offers kindness to all, freely. He can't help but act in accord with his character. But for us to receive his kindness requires having an abiding relationship with him. No abiding, no receiving.

God is infinitely kind. But are we?

Human Kindness

Kindness doesn't denote our character. Neither can we give the blessings of nature nor eternal life to others. But we can develop and demonstrate the character trait of kindness. Following are three of the areas in which the Bible demonstrates human kindness.

Helping People. Kindness demonstrates itself in concrete acts toward people. When kindness abides in our character, we'll aid people in distress and pain. Acts 3 tells of a beggar at the gate of the temple. Crippled from birth and relying on begging for money to support himself, he plied his trade when Peter and John strolled by. Although they didn't have money to give the beggar, they gave what they could. With the simple statement "In the name of Jesus, walk," they eliminated the man's career. He didn't seem to grieve over the loss, but ran and leaped for joy on his newly functioning legs.

Unfortunately, some of the religious leaders didn't share that joy, calling Peter and John on the carpet to explain. In

Acts 4:9, they gladly did: "If we are being called to account today for *an act of kindness* shown to a cripple and are asked how he was healed . . ." (emphasis mine).

Peter declared the healing was an act of kindness. With the Holy Spirit residing within them, they possessed both the kindness and power to share what they had for the beggar's benefit. When the Holy Spirit resides in us, when we allow him to produce his fruit in us, kindness will then change how we treat others. We may not always begin with kindness, we may not always act in kindness, but we'll see more kindness all the time.

The New York Yankees had just endured a tough loss, and the bus ride back to the hotel was quiet and gloomy. Trying to lighten things up, utility infielder Phil Linz picked up his harmonica and played a cheerful tune. Manager Yogi Berra stormed back, berated Linz, and fined him $250. Quite a sum in the days before mega-salaries!

In the off-season, Linz received his contract offer in the mail. Along with a decent raise was a bonus check for $250, with instructions from Berra to spend it on harmonica lessons.

Berra acted in kindness. Kindness doesn't mean we never get upset nor angry but that we make up for it when we do. Kindness is doing the things necessary to get along smoothly with people.

Using Pleasant Language. Our language may be the most difficult area for God to transform. Our learned responses become so automatic we often find it difficult to think before we speak. The quick curse, the angry retort, the frustrated shout seem to flow off our lips. But when kindness permeates our character, 1 Corinthians 4:12-13 promises our language can express it: "We work hard with our own hands. When we are cursed, we bless; when we are persecuted, we endure it; when we are slandered, we *answer kindly*" (emphasis mine).

When people curse us, our kindness allows us to give them better than they gave us. (Better in moral quality, not in quantity of cursing!) When people give us a hard time, our kindness helps us hang in there. When others say bad things about us, we don't retaliate and strike back. Instead, we strive to increase the amount of kindness in the world by our language.

Being Tenderhearted and Forgiving. Kindness allows us to bear with others when they wound us. Kindness and grudge keeping are incompatible: "Be kind and compassionate to one another, forgiving each other, just as in Christ God forgave you" (Ephesians 4:32).

Did you notice the source of kindness and forgiving? We share with others what we receive from God. Because God is kind to us, we desire to be kind to others.

As a teenager, Kari struggled often with her mother. Finally attempting to change, she tried to convince her mother she was now different. The process was slow, and Kari complained to a friend that her mom kept getting historical.

"Don't you mean *hysterical?*" her friend asked.

"No, she's historical. She keeps bringing up the past!"

With God's tenderhearted kindness within us, we don't get historical. We kindly allow people to grow beyond their past.

CULTIVATING KINDNESS

We've seen how kindness is shown both in God and in us, but how do we develop it ourselves?

To establish kindness as a character trait, we need to

follow two steps. First, we need to weed out artificial kindness; then we need to nurture kindness by allowing the presence of God to transform our character.

Weeding Out Self-Serving Kindness

Delilah showed great kindness to Samson, but that kindness was self-serving. In Genesis 25, Jacob kindly gave some stew to his brother, Esau. But that kindness was in exchange for Esau's birthright. In both examples, the giver gave for personal benefit. Like Delilah and Jacob, many of us have learned the best way to get our way is to be nice. In doing things for others, we don't appear to be selfish.

But we keep track of our kindnesses and, when needed, we call in our chips: "Fred, remember when I loaned you $100 to get your car fixed? I've got a little problem. Can you call your friend down at city hall to get my building permit through?"

Is it wrong to ask friends for help? Surely not. That's part of supporting one another. But when we use our acts of kindness as subtle blackmail, that's manipulation.

Flattery and compliments may look similar on the surface, but they're polar opposites. Compliments benefit the receiver; flattery benefits the giver. A gracious, well-chosen compliment can be the essence of kindness, a vital part of the ministry of encouragement. But flattery is selfishness hidden by kindness.

To establish kindness in our character, we must carefully examine our motives to discover the false fruit of self-serving kindness. Since being self-serving comes so naturally, we need to be ruthless in this weeding process. Are our acts of kindness a pure expression of doing what is right, or are they manipulative?

If our motive is selfish, we need to rethink the process.

We should be acting without regard to reward, out of our kind character.

NURTURING THE FRUIT OF KINDNESS

Once we've weeded out selfish kindness, we move on to nurture the growth of kindness in our character. As with all the other character traits we discuss in this book, kindness doesn't usually appear full-grown in our lives. Our role in the partnership with God is to enhance the conditions in the garden of our spirit that aid the development of each trait. The step in doing that is cultivating our closeness to God.

Focus on God's Presence

God is kind, and that kindness is shown in all his actions. As Christians, we reflect the kind character of God. The more we cultivate the presence of God in our lives, through Bible study, prayer, and continual contact with him, the more kindness we'll see in our character. We also need to nurture two specific aspects of God's kindness: the value he places on people, and the commitment to act kindly to build others.

Place a High Value on People. God doesn't act toward us in kindness because our great moral fiber demands it (we're certainly not perfect!). Rather, God sees an innate value within each person, which makes kindness the right thing to do. We don't earn or deserve kindness based on our behavior. But our value as people created by God makes us worthy recipients. We need to develop this same attitude of kindness toward others.

Philippians 4:8 tells us to allow only positive, edifying thoughts. We all have thoughts like, *That jerk deserves to be taught a lesson for cutting me off like that in traffic. I'll show him!* The kind response would be, *That guy sure doesn't deserve kindness. But I don't deserve kindness either. Since I'm a kind person, like my God, I'll treat him with the kindness God uses toward me.*

Radical? Completely. And we can only respond like that when we change our character. That character change comes from consistently looking at people as worthy of kindness — not based on their behavior, but on the value God places on them. If we train ourselves to look at people this way, our attitude toward them will change.

In the 1994 movie *The War,* Kevin Costner plays a Vietnam vet, scarred and traumatized by the brutality of war and killing. His goal in life is to make the world better than he found it, but he grieves because he killed more people than he saved in the war.

The war continues on his return home. His two children experience friction with the six bullying children of another family. While Costner buys cotton candy for his wife and daughter at a fair, his son, played by Elijah Wood, gets beaten up by the bullies once more.

Later, as Costner escorts his bleeding son to their car, he sees two of the youngest children from the other family. He walks over to them and hands them the cotton candy, which they hesitatingly accept. They're not sure just what he's doing, but the lure of candy is irresistible.

His ten-year-old-son is enraged. "Do you know who they are? They're the kids who beat me up!"

"I know that," his dad calmly replies.

"Then why did you give them the candy?"

"Because they look like they haven't been given anything in a long time."

After a series of long and difficult struggles, the son develops the kindness of his father, culminating in a courageous act that transcends all the previous friction. What's the point? That kindness should be given to all, that kindness has the inherent power to transform life.

That's the pattern for us. As we confront a situation, before we act we need to remind ourselves of both the importance of others and our need to act with kindness. That repeated valuing of others will build itself into our character.

Treat People As God Does. Until we value people deeply, we won't be allowed to help them grow. Kindness is the key: "Do not let any unwholesome talk come out of your mouths, but only what is helpful for building others up according to their needs, that it may benefit those who listen. . . . *Be kind and compassionate* to one another, forgiving each other, just as in Christ God forgave you" (Ephesians 4:29, 32, emphasis mine).

Just as God gave of himself to aid our spiritual growth, so we need to involve ourselves in the growth process of others. We can build others up by saying kind things to and about them and by acting in kind ways toward them. When we're kind, we grow in kindness! The emotional part of kindness follows our mental attitude and physical actions. When we pray for people, when we act to help them grow spiritually, kindness grows deeper in our character.

Part of "training ourselves in godliness" is using kind language, refusing to retaliate, tenderheartedly forgiving one another, and valuing people as God does. When we work to build others up, the fruit of kindness grows in our inner person, and we become like our Father.

STEPS TOWARD CHARACTER CHANGE
1. How would you define *kindness*?
2. Does it ever bother you that God is kind to all people, even his enemies? Do you think that's fair? Explain.

3. Describe a time when God showed kindness to you. How did that affect your life and feelings?

4. When was the last time you were kind to someone? Were you kind to be kind, or were you kind for your own benefit? How did your response of kindness make you feel afterward—proud, guilty, etc.?

5. On a scale of 1 to 5, with 1 representing "I have no kindness" and 5 representing "I most often respond with kindness," where would you put yourself? Why?

6. What weeds most threaten to choke out kindness in your life? How can you begin to pull those weeds?

7. When is it most difficult for you to be tenderhearted and forgiving?

8. If someone listened to your conversations, would he or she rate you highly on kind language? What can you do to improve in this area?

9. Based on how kind you are to others, how highly do you think you value others? Give an example.

10. Think of the coming week. To what person or in what situation can you choose to be genuinely kind? Share that decision with someone you trust. Ask that person to hold you accountable to be kind, even when it isn't for your benefit.

CHAPTER 8
Moral Fiber
Goodness

But the fruit of the Spirit is . . . goodness.
—PAUL THE APOSTLE, in GALATIANS 5:22

The title character in the comic strip *Broom Hilda* is an ugly yet somehow lovable witch. Her friend Irwin, the troll, has all the innocence and naïveté needed to be truly attractive. One day Broom Hilda asks, "Irwin, what would be the best way to make the world better?"

Irwin thinks for a moment and replies, "Start with yourself! Give up your bad habits and evil pleasures. Then when you're good, when you're perfect, you'll stand as a shining example to others!"

Broom Hilda swiftly responds, "What's the second best way?"

Most of us want to be good. But not too good—and not all the time. Our age has abandoned moral fiber. We've lost our moral compass, a reliable source of right and wrong, and we drift. In our age of relativism, people choose what's good according to individual desires.

In the 1994–95 football season, a Los Angeles Raiders football player got away with a cheap shot (a late, unnecessary, and intended-to-hurt-the-opponent hit). The camera caught it, the instant replay showed it, but the officials missed it. No penalty was called. As commentators castigated him in the following furor, he replied, "It's only a dirty hit if you get caught. I got away with it." He had his standards of right and wrong, and he felt comfortable with them.

Deep within each person lives the concept of good and evil. Although we may vary in the specifics of what we say is good, we all have inner standards that determine our morality. But we choose our standards. We may choose to accept the standards we've been taught by parents, church, school, and peers, or create our own personal standards. But we decide what is good or evil. We tend to reject the concept of an absolute definition of good from a source outside ourselves.

A 1991 Barna study revealed only 28 percent of Americans strongly believe in absolute truth. More frightening, only 23 percent of evangelical Christians accept absolute truth. Perhaps that explains in part why the behavior of Christians often is worse than the behavior of unbelievers, as the study in chapter 1 of this book disclosed. If we can't find anything that is always true, then our sense of good can change. For example, some may say that sometimes sex outside marriage is wrong, but that sometimes it's acceptable.

In this environment, good is usually what pleases or benefits us and what we have the ability to get away with. But because good isn't the same for all individuals, trying to hold on to what is good compares with trying to grab smoke with our hands.

In contrast, God offers an innate, absolute goodness that flows from his character. When the Holy Spirit lives within, one of his fruits is goodness. By definition, we Christians desire to build that goodness into the core of our character. But that task is made more difficult with the worldly pressures to choose either evil or such a relativistic definition of good that the concept of good loses all meaning.

OUR NATURAL TENDENCY: GO FOR EVIL

Because God is the only source of absolute good, we face four basic options in choosing good and evil in our lives. We can deliberately choose what we know is evil, or we can choose to establish our own standards of good. We can also choose to appear good by God's standards, while at the same time refusing to move toward inner goodness. Lastly, we can choose to be good, as God defines goodness. Of the four, only one chooses absolute goodness; the others, by default if not intent, choose evil. Let's examine each of these options.

Choosing Known Evil

We all have evil within us. Dwight L. Moody once said, "I have had more trouble with myself than any other man I have met." We could all echo Paul's statement in Romans 3:10-13, 23 as we acknowledge our own evil: "'There is no one righteous, not even one; there is no one who understands, no one who seeks God. All have turned away, they have together become worthless; there is no one who does good, not even one.' . . . For all have sinned and fall short of the glory of God."

But some people major in evil. It dominates their character. Evil people recognize right and wrong, and knowingly choose the wrong. They believe the benefits of evil outweigh the disadvantages and think the consequences will never catch up to them. A wine commercial expresses this view by saying (paraphrased), "No man goes before his time. Unless, of course, the boss leaves early." Good is what you can get away with.

Others believe the advantages of evil exceed the costs, even if they are caught. For example, they would be willing to rob a bank of $5 million, hide the money, get caught, and then serve ten years in prison in order to be rich when they get out!

When continually repeated, evil choices callous a person's conscience until it's functionally dead. While all people make some evil choices, others choose it so frequently they begin to personify evil. Charles Manson and Adolph Hitler are two who appear to be in this group.

Choosing Our Own Standard of Good

Probably the largest of the four groups include those who want to be good, but by their own definition: *I'm a decent person, so God couldn't keep me out of heaven. I'm not perfect, but I've never killed anyone. I'm faithful to my wife. The only time I cheat is with the IRS, and that really doesn't count.* Maybe I don't go to church, but I worship God in my own way.

Doing good things does show some goodness in people. But it's not enough. People who want to be good by their own definition possess no solution to the evil that still lives within them. They try to establish their own righteousness (see Romans 10:3). The inadequacy of their situation is described in Ephesians 2:8-9: "For it is by grace you have been saved, through faith —*and this not from yourselves*, it is the gift of God —*not by works*, so that no one can boast" (emphasis mine).

Although such people don't intentionally or knowingly choose evil, they don't choose God's good and thus end up in evil's camp.

Choosing the Appearance of Good

Hypocrites want to appear good while still doing evil. The word *hypocrite* comes from the Greek word for an actor. Before the days of binoculars and opera glasses, dramas were often performed in large amphitheaters. Because crucial facial expressions couldn't be seen, the actor would hold up a mask. A mask with a smiling face showed comedy or happiness. A mask with a frowning face denoted tragedy or sadness. Today, our symbol for acting combines these two masks of comedy and tragedy.

But in time the word acquired a moral meaning: those who want to appear different on the outside than they are on the inside. Hypocrites want to look good and do evil:

> Woe to you, teachers of the law and Pharisees, you hypocrites! You are like whitewashed tombs, which look beautiful on the outside but on the inside are full of dead men's bones and everything unclean. In the same way, on the outside you appear to people as righteous but on the inside you are full of hypocrisy and wickedness. (Matthew 23:27-28)

I believe these are the lukewarm believers of Revelation 3:14-16, whom Jesus will spit out of his mouth.

God doesn't want anything to do with people who only want to appear good while holding onto evil. He abhors that intellectual dishonesty. But there is another option.

Choosing God's Goodness
Some choose deep-down goodness, an absolute goodness defined by God. These people want to do what's right and good. They don't claim perfection, but they have a passion to get closer to it.

Probably the smallest of all four groups, this group is our focus: those who commit their lives to goodness and are willing to pay the price. They deeply desire the Christian character trait of goodness.

THE CHRISTIAN CHARACTER
TRAIT OF GOODNESS
God wants us to be good deep down in our character rather

than just "doing some good things." He desires that we possess a holy passion for purity.

Goodness Defined

Goodness is a deep-seated desire to be upright, virtuous, praiseworthy, pure, and holy. That's quite a task for a sinful human! But our desire to have this trait embedded in our inner person is the key. For many, goodness is whatever they decide is good. For the Christian, goodness flows from God's character. God defines goodness by who he is and gives us biblical examples of people who sought after the Christian character trait of goodness.

Examples of God's Goodness. Matthew 19:16-17 offers several insights about God, including a statement of unity between the Father and the Son. But the main point reveals the goodness of God the Father: "Now a man came up to Jesus and asked, 'Teacher, what good thing must I do to get eternal life?' 'Why do you ask me about what is good?' Jesus replied. 'There is *only One who is good.* If you want to enter life, obey the commandments'" (emphasis mine).

Jesus proclaims that goodness both fills God's character, and flows from God. God doesn't just *do* good things; he *is* good.

We're not like that. We do good things, but goodness doesn't fill us, driving out the evil within. As someone once said, "There's always some bad in the best of us, and always some good in the worst of us." But God wants to get that process of becoming good started in our lives. As we desire to be filled with the goodness of God and allow him to begin the process, we develop goodness in our character.

Examples of Good People. The Bible records several examples of individuals who became so involved in the "growing toward goodness" process that they were described as good.

In Matthew 25, Jesus tells the story of the three workers who had each been given some of the owner's property to use and develop for the benefit of the owner. The first two did well, investing for a return of profit on the principal. But the third was afraid to fail, merely hiding the money so it wouldn't be stolen. When the owner returned to settle accounts, he evaluated the work of the first two by saying, "Well done, *good* and faithful servant!" (verses 21 and 23, emphasis mine).

What made those servants good? An active passion to do what the owner wanted. They established a goal for their lives: to work for the benefit of the owner. Then they used what they had to reach the goal. They were faithful in carrying it out.

But the third wasn't praised. In verse 26 he was called wicked and lazy, the opposite of good. Lazy I can understand. But wicked? There's no record of embezzlement, fraud, or immorality. So why was he wicked? Because he did nothing to advance the cause of the owner. Being evil means to work against God, either actively or passively, by refusing to work for him.

Merely avoiding the more noticeable expressions of sin isn't enough. Goodness is positive action, not merely refraining from sin. If we passionately and actively do what God desires, we are on our way to cultivating the trait of goodness.

Barnabas demonstrated that principle. Acts 11 reveals how some of the Christians who were scattered by the persecution of Stephen went to Antioch and established a new church. The apostles in Jerusalem sent Barnabas there to check out the situation, and he became a source of great encouragement. Soon he recruited the former archenemy of the church, Saul of Tarsus, to work with him. Barnabas is described as "a good man, full of the Holy Spirit and faith" (verse 24). What made him good?

First, he willingly worked for God, going anywhere and doing anything God led him to do. His entire life was committed to encouraging people in the faith. He even stood up to his close missionary partner Paul when he believed Paul wasn't showing enough forgiveness to John Mark.

Second, Barnabas took a stand against his own self-interest. In Acts 4 he sacrificially gave a field he owned to the church to provide for the needy. He was willing to give up what was his for the benefit of others.

Third, he encouraged people spiritually. Although he was originally known as Joseph, the apostles were so impressed with how he encouraged others that they called him Barnabas, literally meaning "Son of Encouragement." The nickname stuck for the rest of his life because he continued to live it out.

Fourth, Barnabas allowed God's Spirit to fill his life. He earnestly desired to be the best God designed him to be, and all his actions came from his faith.

Seeking after goodness means allowing God to fill your life with his good character, giving your life to God so he may use it as he desires, and accepting God's standards for right and wrong.

CULTIVATING GOODNESS

To nurture a productive garden where the fruit of goodness can flourish, we need to eliminate anything that works against the growth of our character trait. Two noxious weeds must be pulled out.

Weeding Out Evil

Most of us have at least started to move away from evil. We have done so either because of our interest in, or our commitment to, God. We've expressed a desire for good in reading this book. But we need to step more fully toward goodness by deciding to "avoid every kind of evil" (1 Thessalonians 5:22).

We don't wake up one morning and decide, *Today, evil is gone from my life, fully and forever,* and expect that decision alone to completely and permanently remove evil. Rather, we must work continually, beginning with a conscious decision to weed out evil.

We'll never truly want to weed out evil until we deeply understand how evil evil is. Evil appears good. If it didn't, why would so many people do so much of it? Second Corinthians 11:14 tells us, "Satan himself masquerades as an angel of light." But the benefits of sin don't last. Although sin has pleasure for a short time (see Hebrews 11:25), in the long run it destroys our lives.

We need to establish an abhorrence of evil, stemming from our recognition of its destructive power. Romans 12:9 tells us, "Love must be sincere. *Hate what is evil;* cling to what is good" (emphasis mine). The only way we can cling to what is good is to decide, with our will, to hate evil and move away. There's a reason God's Spirit is called the *Holy* Spirit. For us to develop the character traits of God through the fruit of the Spirit, we need to weed out our desire for evil. Over time, we become more sensitive to the Holy Spirit's teaching and correcting and convicting us. We respond to those hopefully gentle nudges with growing holiness.

If you're in the process of becoming good, don't expect overnight miracles. Be patient. Remember, it didn't take

113

our Lord long to get his people out of Egypt. But it took forty years to get Egypt out of his people.

We begin with our decision to seek good and to avoid every form of evil. We repeat that promise to ourselves daily, take courage from our victories, and confess our losses. We continue to stand against evil.

Shane struggled with pornography. While traveling a lot for his own business, temptations were ample and successful. The temptation then grew with a new job, which required him to monitor incoming mail, some of which was porn. No longer did he have to visit a store to see it; now it was in his hands. Resisting the desire to open the pages was like holding back an ocean wave with a plastic rake.

Shane grew disgusted with himself at losing the spiritual battles. He didn't like the attitudes viewing porn brought, and he began to hate the evil more than he enjoyed the pleasures it produced. By taking a stand against evil, he learned how to short-circuit the process. At the first opportunity, before temptation built its irresistible pressure, he just said no. With a decision of his will backed by the power of the Holy Spirit, Shane finally began to win battles. He still loses some, but the losses are fewer all the time. He took a stand against evil and saw goodness grow.

Weeding Out Hypocrisy

Hypocrisy is wanting to appear good, without paying the price of eliminating evil in our lives. Hypocrisy means we intentionally and continually don't desire to be the same on the inside as we are on the outside.

Physics professor Dr. Malcolm Smedley had given the same lecture hundreds of times. Each time his old chauffeur, Joe, listened in. One night Joe told the professor that he thought he could do the lecture just as well. Dr. Smedley didn't believe him but was willing to let him try. So they changed clothing.

The chauffeur gave a flawless lecture that received a standing ovation. Then the master of ceremonies said, "We have a little time left. With the permission of our honored guest, perhaps we can spend that in a question-and-answer session." Although the chauffeur couldn't even understand what the first question was about, he was quick on his feet. He replied, "I'm surprised such a simple question would even be asked in such a learned assembly. That question is so basic, I'm going to ask my chauffeur to come up and answer it."

Our hypocrisy probably won't have such an easy solution! The true solution to hypocrisy is realizing that the evil we think we hide really isn't hidden at all. Hebrews 4:13 tells us, "Nothing in all creation is hidden from God's sight." But what Jesus said in another passage causes even more fear in hypocrites:

> Be on your guard against the yeast of the Pharisees, which is hypocrisy. There is nothing concealed that will not be disclosed, or hidden that will not be made known. What you have said in the dark will be heard in the daylight, and what you have whispered in the ear in the inner rooms will be proclaimed from the roofs. (Luke 12:1-3)

God sees and discloses our internal reality. That totally eliminates hypocrisy, the intentional difference between the outward appearance of good and inner clinging to evil. If our heart desires to be good, we weed out the evil of hypocrisy with an honest confession of who we are: a normal human, struggling with sin, who wants to become good. We are transparent before God and man, not pretending to be better than we are.

We need help from others in doing this. One of the greatest reasons for hypocrisy is the fear that if others really knew the evil within us, they couldn't love and accept us. So as we love others unconditionally, as we accept them with their imperfections, we give them the freedom to share with minimized risk.

Christians are intended to be wounded healers, working together toward goodness by admitting the evil within. Ironically, only as we admit our evil can we experience victory over it and begin to replace evil with good.

NURTURING THE FRUIT OF GOODNESS

Since goodness doesn't come naturally, we must learn what goodness truly is. As we study the words of God and see his heart, we nurture good in our lives.

The Words of God

Our conscience is a product of whatever we program into it, our own definition of what is good. If a person follows his own standards of right and wrong, his conscience will give him no trouble. In fact, it will congratulate him on being a fine, moral person. But his standards may not match at all what God establishes as good.

We need something deeper, more reliable, and consistent: a solid, absolute source of morality that can come only from the nature of God. Second Timothy 3:16-17 promises that all we need for complete spiritual lives is found in the Bible. As we learn God's definition of good, we need to implant it in our consciences.

The Bible yields two types of passages that reveal what is good: general principles and specific commands. Jesus' statement in Matthew 22 that we must love God and love people is a general principle. Specific commands, such as the prohibition of sexual intercourse outside marriage, are examples of the best way to express the general principle of love in that specific situation. When we're faced with a moral choice, we look in the Bible to discover what God calls good in the situation, either from principle or command. We don't rely on our untaught natural conscience, our emotions, our preference, or what others have taught us, because these sources are all too vulnerable to serve as primary sources of good.

The Bible establishes the foundation for morality, for knowing the difference between right and wrong. The more we know the Bible, the more we know what God calls good. This is the beginning point as we program our conscience with this.

But we need to go beyond merely learning what the Bible says about a situation. In our contemporary, technological world, often no biblical command or principle applies clearly. What's most moral regarding in vitro fertilization? genetic engineering? These issues are never addressed specifically in the Bible. That's why we need to move beyond the letter of the law to the spirit of the law.

The Heart of God
When we can't find a command or principle for determining good, we can discover and rely on the heart of God. God's heart has an absolute purity toward good and an absolute revulsion toward evil. This knowledge of the heart of God comes with maturity, based on a thorough knowledge of the Bible and a long-term walk with God.

Hebrews 5:14 explains it this way: "But solid food is for the mature, who by *constant use* have trained themselves to *distinguish good from evil"* (emphasis mine). We begin with "milk," evaluating each situation in light of what the Bible specifically teaches about good. By the "constant use" of running each case through the filter of what the Bible teaches as good, we then train ourselves to recognize the difference between good and evil. Over time, that procedure gives us an inner sense of right and wrong, because God's heart is in us, building into us his character trait of goodness. We begin to "do what Jesus would do."

We commit to grow in the character trait of goodness when we determine to do what's good, regardless of the cost. As we cooperate with God, allowing him to chip away anything that doesn't match his standard of goodness, the final product is a character filled with goodness, with moral fiber.

When I stand at the throne of God, I desire to hear Jesus say, "Well done, *good* and faithful servant. Come and share your master's happiness." How about you?

STEPS TOWARD CHARACTER CHANGE

1. How do you define *goodness?*
2. Do you think the concept of absolute truth is essential to developing goodness? Why or why not?
3. What aspect of God's goodness most intrigues you?
4. Is there a person in your life you think of as "good"? If so, what makes you think that?
5. Describe a situation, either from your own life or someone you know (please leave out the person's name), that exemplifies each of the four ways of approaching evil:
   - choosing known evil

- choosing your own standards of good
- choosing the appearance of good
- choosing God's goodness

6. Which approach most exemplifies your life? In what ways is it difficult for you to choose deep-down goodness?

7. On a scale of 1 to 5, with 1 representing "I have no goodness" and 5 representing "I most often respond with goodness," where would you place yourself? Why?

8. What weeds threaten to choke out goodness in your life? How can you begin to pull those weeds?

9. In the upcoming month, make a promise to God that you will spend time every day reading your Bible. Share that promise with someone you trust, and ask him or her to call you once a week to hold you accountable as you grow in goodness.

CHAPTER 9

Keeping Commitments

Faithfulness

But the fruit of the Spirit is . . . faithfulness.
— PAUL THE APOSTLE, in GALATIANS 5:22

Sharon's dream was simple: to marry Nick, her high-school sweetheart, to have children, and to grow old together, as a family. But the marriage vows disintegrated when Nick realized many other relationships were available. He felt confined in just one.

With his decision, Sharon's lifetime dreams crashed. Her worst nightmares had never put her in the role of a divorced woman, and she struggled with her self-image. Because Nick was too busy playing to spend time with them, Sharon's two boys grew up without their dad. Financially, she was pinched; although she worked full time, they still had to live in a government-subsidized apartment. Why did this happen? Someone broke their commitment.

Little Johnny had just moved to town with his folks, and with great eagerness they visited a local church. Johnny arrived early so he wouldn't miss anything and was taken to the Sunday school room. There he waited, and waited, and waited, for the teacher to show up. Just at the scheduled time she rushed in, greeted the kids, and presented a hastily thrown-together lesson on how we should love God with all our heart. But Johnny and his parents never went back to that church. Why? Someone broke their commitment.

One of the character changes God wants to make in us deals with faithfulness. Faithfulness that will impact our marriages. Faithfulness that will impact our churches. Faithfulness that will impact our words and our work. God wants us to be people of integrity, who keep our commitments. Why is it then that, although 60 percent of Americans claim to be Christians, only 40 percent regularly attend church? And even within the church, only half of the total members attend worship each week. What's the problem? Unfaithfulness.

OUR NATURAL TENDENCY: UNFAITHFULNESS

Unfaithfulness runs through the Old Testament book of Malachi. The people of Israel returned from the Babylonian captivity to Jerusalem and rebuilt the temple. But they never finished the protective walls of the city. In addition, their overall religious practice declined. What was at the core of this unfaithfulness? The leaders, according to Malachi 2:7-9:

> "For the lips of a priest ought to preserve knowledge, and from his mouth men should seek instruction — because he is the messenger of the Lord Almighty. But you have turned from the way and by your teaching have caused many to stumble; you have violated the covenant with Levi," says the Lord Almighty. "So I have caused you to be despised and humiliated before all the people, because you have not followed my ways but have shown partiality in matters of the law."

The leaders failed to live up to their commitment to be spiritual guides. As you read through Malachi, you'll see that they consistently offered poor quality in serving God.

Many leaders today also break faith. After several years as an associate minister, Nolan was being interviewed for the position of senior pastor at another church. A discerning elder asked the young minister how long he planned to stay. With firmness and a winning smile, he said he wanted to finish out his ministry there. He brought eagerness, enthusiasm, and skill in preaching. He and the church fit together well. The church grew in numbers and in health.

Then a larger church heard of his preaching ability and called him as their pastor. He truly believed God was leading. Surely the greater salary to take care of his growing family was confirmation. But reality at the new church didn't quite match what he had been told, and he longed for "the good old days." During this time, his former church brought in a "seasoned minister," someone who truly would end his ministry there, and provide stability.

Unfortunately, that minister just wanted to quietly finish out his time before retirement, and the church lost its momentum. Why? People broke their commitments.

When leaders break faith in serving God, people follow: "Have we not all one Father? Did not one God create us? Why do *we profane the covenant* of our fathers by *breaking faith* with one another?" (Malachi 2:10, emphasis mine).

Malachi 2–3 specifically shows how Judah broke faith: by intermarriage with unbelievers (2:11), by rampant divorce (2:13-15), with physical abuse of spouses (2:16), and by failure to tithe (3:8-10). That sounds suspiciously like the church today. We're plagued by the same sins. A November 1994 article in the Riverside *Press-Enterprise* estimated that only five thousand families nationwide tithe. While I believe that figure is greatly understated, nearly all would agree tithing is not the norm in church life.

God doesn't take unfaithfulness lightly. Just as he keeps his commitments, he expects us to keep ours. In Malachi 2:1-3, when the leaders broke faith, they experienced the consequences:

> "And now this admonition is for you, O priests. If you do not listen, and if you do not set your heart to honor my name," says the Lord Almighty, "I will send a curse upon you, and I will curse your blessings. . . . Because of you I will rebuke your descendants; I will spread on your faces the offal from your festival sacrifices."

Malachi 3:2-3 extends similar consequences to the people who break faith: "But who can endure the day of his coming? Who can stand when he appears? For he will be like a refiner's fire or a launderer's soap. . . . Then the Lord will have men who will bring offerings in righteousness."

God will not put up with unfaithfulness forever because commitments are of vital importance to him. At some time in our lives, all of us have been unfaithful to God, our families, our churches, our employers, ourselves. But by his Spirit living in us, God wants to change our character to one of faithfulness.

THE CHRISTIAN CHARACTER TRAIT OF FAITHFULNESS

All of us keep some commitments; we also fail to keep some. We tend to keep those that are easy to keep, that benefit us—at least until we change our minds. But God wants to take our sporadic faithfulness and transform us so that faithfulness is who we are deep down.

God yearns for us to be people who want to keep commitments, who work at keeping commitments, and who cooperate with him in accomplishing that.

Faithfulness Defined

Very simply, faithfulness is keeping our word. Following through on commitments. Being reliable. Not changing every moment based on the current trend or our advantage. Faithfulness means we place a high value on keeping our promises, that our word is our bond. If we say something, people know they can rely on us because we don't waffle on our word.

Mel was a worker, always on the go, continually finding an extra job to bring in more money. But that desire for more soon took over. During the week he spent his time as a carpenter, and as a side business, he hired out to mow large fields with his tractor. He agreed with his neighbor Jack to mow a field of wild mustard and weeds for one hundred dollars, but other jobs got in the way. Despite Jack's calls, he kept putting it off.

When Mel finally got ready, he informed Jack the cost would be two hundred dollars, since the weeds had gotten larger with thicker stems and would require two passes. Mel thought he had Jack in a bind, since the deadline set by the fire department for mowing was almost up, and he knew that Jack couldn't find anyone else at such a late date. So he figured on an easy extra hundred dollars.

But Jack figured Mel had broken the original agreement. Of the two, Jack was right. Mel broke faith. And Mel claimed to be a Christian; they went to the same church (when Mel wasn't working on a side job, that is).

Faithfulness gives us integrity to do the right thing, regardless of personal cost. We carry out our commitments; we sacrifice to keep our promise. We do what we say. That kind of integrity comes only from God.

God's Faithfulness

Psalm 89 proclaims the faithfulness of God: "I will sing of the Lord's great love forever; with my mouth I will make your faithfulness known through all generations. I will declare that your love stands firm forever, that you established your faithfulness in heaven itself" (verses 1-2).

Faithfulness flows from the nature of God. Even when we're unfaithful, God remains true to his commitments. Second Timothy 2:11-13 gives a fascinating insight into the character of God and our relationship with him: "Here is a trustworthy saying: If we died with him, we will also live with him; if we endure, we will also reign with him. If we disown him, he will also disown us; if we are faithless, *he will remain faithful*, for he cannot disown himself" (emphasis mine).

Paul is saying that if we disown God or withdraw from being his child, God will in turn disown us or break the relationship. But if we are faithless, God will still live up to the promises he's made to us, for he cannot be unfaithful to himself. If we confess our sins, God will welcome us back like the Prodigal Son. He will be faithful to forgive and restore us. God won't change the rules during the game.

When I was in junior high, I had a teacher with whom I clashed. At the start of the semester, he told us the requirements to receive each grade. Since I needed a B to stay in an honor group, I was careful to meet the minimum requirements.

Then, one week before midterm grades came out, he

changed the rules. The new rules gave me a C, and it was too late to move it up to a B. I was enraged at the unfairness of it because I knew the change was directed at me. It knocked me out of the honor group.

I vowed revenge. I made arrangements with the counselor to transfer out of the class at semester break and put my plan into effect. This particular teacher had a facial tic, where he would grimace about once a minute. Each time he glanced my way I would look him in the eye and make that same facial tic. When he tried not to look at me, I learned to stretch my arms to attract his attention. I would get him, again and again. Other students caught on and enjoyed the tweaking of authority's nose, too. I knew I could deny doing anything if I were ever called on it, and I only had a few weeks to go before I was out of his class.

Then I learned my greatest lesson. Even when teachers are wrong, they still have power. For some strange reason, the counselor changed his mind about allowing me to transfer out. It had to do with learning to get along with difficult people and not running.

Was I a better-behaved student the next semester? Of course. I wasn't completely stupid. There were no more facial tics on my part, no more intentional provoking. But to this day, over thirty years later, his unfaithfulness is remembered. I've forgiven him, and if I were to meet him today I would ask his forgiveness for being so rude and inconsiderate. My behavior was inexcusable. But forgiveness doesn't mask how wrong he was to be unfaithful to the rules.

Thankfully, God won't do that. He's faithful to his promises. If he says something, he'll stick with it—even when we go through patterns of sinning. When you have the opportunity, read the Old Testament book of Judges, a gracious twenty-one-chapter story of forgiveness. The pattern stayed the same: The nation of Israel would forsake God and cling to evil; God would turn them over to their enemies; then the people would come to their senses, repent, and ask God to take them back. And each time he did. Over and over again.

I can't tell you how much I appreciate God's faithfulness because I often get stuck in the same pattern as that of the Israelites. And my guess is that you do, too. We *need* the faithfulness of God.

Personally, I'm glad that someone with faithfulness embedded in their character is the Lord of creation. If I were to experience the repeated betrayals God has endured, I don't think I would have responded as he does. This would more likely be my response: "You've pushed me too far this time. I know I said I would forgive you if you repented, but I never thought you would do it this often! From now on, we're changing the rules. One more mistake on your part, and you're dead."

I could see me doing that. But God won't. Why? Because he keeps the commitments he makes. That's who he is; that's his character. And his people can have that character, too.

Faithfulness: Expected of God's People

Faithfulness applies only to commitments we make, so only those who make commitments to God are held accountable for keeping them. God doesn't require those with no faith to keep faith. But have no doubt, God expects Christians to be faithful: "Now it is required that those who have been given a trust *must prove faithful*" (1 Corinthians 4:2, emphasis mine).

We've been entrusted with the ability to grow spiritually. We've been entrusted with a ministry, a way to serve God, that is unique to each of us. Are we faithful to God, our families, our church, our bosses, ourselves in the trust we've accepted?

None of us will ever be fully faithful, and God does forgive. Rather than perfect faithfulness, God requires a passion for faithfulness. That doesn't mean we never fail. But when a faithful person fails, he acknowledges it to God and to the individuals he's broken faith with. Then he picks up the pieces and moves on, rebuilding his reputation as a faithful person.

Faithfulness is difficult. It requires saying no to ourselves in order to keep our word. It means sometimes doing without, in order to pay the bills we committed to pay. But God calls us to cultivate faithfulness in our character.

CULTIVATING FAITHFULNESS

In his comic strip, character Andy Capp (a lovable Cockney rogue) strolls up to the neighborhood pub and apologizes to his waiting friend: "Sorry I'm a bit late, Chalkie, but I was spinnin' a coin t' decide whether I should spend the morning playin' billiards or spend it lookin' for a job."

Chalkie smiles. "An' billiards won, eh?"

Andy replies, "Yep, but it took about fifteen throws!"

As human beings, we do what we want to do. We analyze the options, calculate the cost/benefit ratio, and choose what's most important to us. Sometimes we go through amazing verbal rationalizations just to do what we want. But that process can also be used to build faithfulness. The key is to prioritize our lives, determining, most of all, that we want to live up to our commitments and be a person of our word. Then we can work to eliminate whatever works against faithfulness.

Weeding Out Short-Term Thinking

For many of us, our wisdom extends no further than a week. We substitute short-term solutions to problems that at best have a long-term character solution. What do I mean? Here's an example.

Let's say we've made a number of financial commitments, including our mortgage, that have us stretched to the limit. We get laid off from work and live off credit cards for several months. Soon, even though we're back at work, we've got such debt that we would have to win the lottery to pay it all off.

We hear of a bankruptcy attorney. When he explains the options, eliminating our debt looks like instant financial health again. But we tend to ignore two issues. First, bankruptcies have negative long-term financial consequences. Second, and much more important, we made a commitment to pay these bills. We received something of value, and we agreed to pay for it. As Christians, God expects us to live up to our commitments.

If we make decisions like the one above without tremendous consideration and prayer and choose to focus only on short-term benefits, we lose pieces of our character. In the long term, little events either build or destroy our faithfulness.

Remember Mel, who charged Jack another hundred dollars to mow his field? Well, since Jack was in a bind, he paid the extra money. Mel thought he had won, that he had manipulated the situation masterfully. But they lived in a rural area, where people rely on one another and where few secrets live long. Many of the neighbors, who had planned on hiring Mel, saw through his trick into his character. In the short term, he made an extra hundred dollars. In the long term, he lost far more: additional finances and his reputation for faithfulness.

If you want to build faithfulness into your character, weed out short-term benefits and look instead at nurturing long-term character impact.

NURTURING THE FRUIT OF FAITHFULNESS

As with all the character traits, we need to take concrete action in building faithfulness. Our partnership with God provides the foundation by teaching us how to focus on God's faithfulness. Then we can take steps to let his character sink deep down into every aspect of our lives.

Faithfully Fearful of God

Many people get fired up about faithfulness at a rally or conference but don't continue to live faithfully. In effect, they place a higher long-term value on pleasing themselves. But when we value the presence of God in our lives above all else, faithfulness follows: "He gave them these orders: 'You *must serve faithfully* and wholeheartedly *in the fear of the Lord*'" (2 Chronicles 19:9, emphasis mine).

Faithfulness is linked to the fear of God. How does that work? When we recognize the transcendence of God, a normal response is to feel overwhelmed and intimidated; we feel the fear of the Lord. Then, as we realize that God surpasses all else in life, being faithful to him becomes important. Since he's much bigger and more awesome than we are, we desire to please him.

To my immature thirteen-year-old reasoning, that junior-high science teacher was no better than I and certainly didn't deserve my faithfulness. But I had no problem being faithful to other teachers who impressed me greatly with their care, education, and fairness.

In starting the process of becoming faithful deep down, the key distinction deals with the quality of the person

131

we're faithful to. We begin with faithfulness where it's easy to be faithful. Then we extend faithfulness to those who don't deserve it (such as my teacher).

Faithfulness begins with realizing just who lives inside us: the Creator of all. As we nurture the presence of God within us, we grow in trust and faithfulness, and it becomes easier to obey God.

Obedience to God is vital because the Bible links trust and faith with obedience. Deuteronomy 9:23-24 is one example:

> And when the Lord sent you out from Kadesh Barnea, he said, "Go up and take possession of the land I have given you." But you rebelled against the command of the Lord your God. You did not *trust him or obey him.* You *have been rebellious* against the Lord ever since I have known you. (emphasis mine)

God gave the Israelites the land and commanded them to possess it. But in rebellion, they were unfaithful. Although they were God's people, they neither trusted nor obeyed God. In effect, they had no active, deep-down faith in God. A. W. Tozer made this principle clear when he wrote, "The Bible recognizes no faith that does not lead to obedience, nor does it recognize any obedience that does not spring from faith. The two are opposite sides of the same coin."

When people accept Christ, they make a covenant with God to be faithful. Basically, a covenant is a mutual agreement: You do this; I'll do that. As Christians, our part of the covenant is to put God number one in our lives, to obediently follow him, to know him deeply. God's part is to give us abundant forgiveness and grace now, and heaven later.

When we don't come through on our part, we break our

faith covenant with God and compromise our integrity. But when we obey, we are saying, "God, I believe with all my heart that you know what's best for me. So I'll do whatever you tell me, even if it doesn't make sense to me, even if I can't see any benefit now." Obedience can be a fiery crucible that burns away unfaithfulness and brings us closer to him.

Faithfulness toward Others

Our growth in faithfulness must extend to people as well. We cannot show our faithfulness to God without it impacting others. So often we value others for what they do—especially for us. But when we see little value in people, keeping our commitments to them becomes less important. So if they mistreat us, they don't deserve our faithfulness. But if they treat us nicely, then we can be faithful to them.

Fortunately, God always treats people faithfully—not in response to their behavior, but in line with their inherent value as his creations. When we see people with the value God places on them, keeping our commitments to them becomes easier.

In Matthew 25:40, Jesus taught that whatever we do to others, we do to him. Why is that? Our attitude to God's creation (primarily people, but this can include the physical universe as well), reflects our attitude to the Creator. We can't love God if we don't love his people.

If we desire to treat God with faithfulness, we need faithfulness in our relationships. When we tell others we'll pray for them, we better pray for them. If we commit to doing something, we better not only do it, but do the best we're capable of. And if something more exciting comes up, we must explain that we have a previous commitment. If we purchase something on credit, we promise to pay for it, and we do. If we break faith with people, we break faith with God. And we sacrifice the integrity of our relationship with God.

For us to grow in faithfulness, we need to view ourselves as people of value and integrity, bound by our promises. As Jesus said in Matthew 5:33-37, people should be able to rely on our word. Why should we be like that? Because we are children of the King, a faithful king who created us to be faithful.

A lovely villa rests on the shores of beautiful Lake Como in the Italian Alps. Some tourists complimented the trusted old gardener who had maintained the grounds for years.

"The owner must come here frequently," one said.

"No," he replied. "He has been here only once in fifteen years, and then I did not see him."

"But how do you get your orders?"

"From the owner's agent, who lives in Milan."

"Then he must come here often?"

"No, not often. Perhaps once a year or so."

The tourist was amazed. "You have no one to supervise your work, and the grounds are as neat as if you expected the owner to come back tomorrow!"

The old gardener firmly replied, "Today, sir! Not tomorrow, but today."

That gardener was faithful to his trust. May we choose to be just as faithful, to our Lord, and one another.

STEPS TOWARD CHARACTER CHANGE

1. Has someone broken faith with you? If so, describe the situation. How did that make you feel? In what ways did that break in faith change your relationship?
2. List the character traits of a faithful person.

3. Describe a time when God has been faithful to you. Did that situation change your relationship with him in any way? If so, how?

4. On a scale of 1 to 5, with 1 representing "I have no faithfulness" and 5 representing "I most often respond with faithfulness," where would you place yourself? Why?

5. When is it most difficult for you to be faithful? What can you do to improve?

6. Does the presence of God in your life help you to be more faithful? Why or why not?

7. Do you give different values to different people? If so, what standards do you use?

8. How does your value of others around you—your friends, spouse, coworkers, boss, fellow church members—affect your faithfulness toward them? In what relationships should you make a change in your faith attitude?

9. List ten people with whom you spend time and, next to their names, the ways in which you treat each person. Are you being faithful? Ask someone you trust to go over your list with you and give you perspective. Discuss specific steps you can take with at least one of those people in order to allow faithfulness to grow in your life. Then pray, asking God to help you carry out those faithful steps in the coming week.

CHAPTER 10

Choosing Our Response

Gentleness

But the fruit of the Spirit is . . . gentleness.
—PAUL THE APOSTLE, in GALATIANS 5:23

Ever since my teens, I've been a long-suffering fan of the Los Angeles Rams, even through unpopular coaches and owners, overpaid and pampered players, and many losses—including the Super Bowl. I'm intrigued by the strategy of the game, motivated by the physical challenges, and enthused with the sporadic wins.

But I never came so close to getting in a fight as I did when I attended a game two seasons ago. While I was standing in line for a hot dog and a Coke, a man in his twenties, just in front of me, became verbally abusive to the server. He tried to buy more beers than he was allowed and, overall, was obnoxious. Apparently these weren't his first beers of the day. For some reason, he started in on me. (Maybe it was my gentle encouragement to give the server some slack!)

Perhaps he saw a graying man in his forties and figured I was an easy mark. But his foul language and challenge to fight provoked a surprising response in me. He didn't realize this forty-four-year-old had been working out and was stronger than he had ever been. I had also had some training in boxing when I was younger. So I calmly measured the kid and knew I could take him.

I planned the first, second, and third punches. My conscience wouldn't allow me to throw the first punch, but I knew just the words to push him over the edge. Most surprisingly, I wanted to. I don't know if the physical environment of football played a part in that desire, or whether it was a test of my new strength, or increased levels of testosterone from working out. But most likely, it was just my earthly nature. I wanted to teach this young punk a lesson in politeness by flattening him.

But deeper down, I wanted to be gentle, not responding automatically with my old nature. Fortified by urgent and quick prayer, I held back. The onlookers later complimented me on "doing the right thing." But more than their praise I desired the praise of God.

That was a tough situation for me because I'm not a gentle person by nature. Gentleness has been cultivated in my life only with great difficulty. While in elementary school, I formed and led a gang with my best friend, Rocky, against some school bullies. I fought frequently.

Our world is harsh, and gentleness is rarely found. Football games demonstrate that harshness with their ferocious tackles and blocks. Each evening's news brings reports of violence inflicted on people, from Somalia and Bosnia to our own streets. Violence seems to be part of society's fabric.

But God offers an alternative, the Christian character trait of gentleness. The Greek word for this fruit of the Spirit is also translated into the English words *meekness* or *humility*. God allows us to change our inner person so we can consistently choose to respond to the difficulties of life with gentleness. But that's not natural for most of us.

OUR NATURAL TENDENCY: CONFLICT, CONTROL, FEAR, AND SELFISHNESS

Pursuing the character trait of gentleness will change us in four areas of natural response: conflict, control, fear, and selfishness.

Conflict

When faced with conflict, we often respond by attempting to overpower others. Depending on age, attractiveness, physical strength, or intelligence, the tools we use to do that will differ. But our underlying attitude is, *No one pushes me around! I don't get mad, I get even.* That was my initial attitude at the football game, and it's embedded in our world. We don't naturally respond with gentleness, nor do we expect it in others.

While taking an accident report, a Los Angeles police officer asked the driver of the car how he happened to hit the pedestrian on the crosswalk. The driver replied, "I didn't touch him. I saw him in the crosswalk, came to a stop, motioned for him to cross, and he fainted."

Gentleness in conflict is so rare. We tend to use force even if we have an alternative because power is quicker, sometimes easier, and certainly requires less self-control. But gentleness gives us a better option in dealing with conflict.

Can you imagine the headlines if I hadn't finally brought gentleness to the football game: "Christian minister arrested for brawling at Rams' game. Film at eleven"?

Control

We also need gentleness to combat our normal desire to be in charge. We tend to discount others, to treat their needs and wounds as not being as important as ours. We can run over people, even when our goals are good. We can be

139

much too forceful to those who seem to oppose what we want to do in life. For instance, we may want to give to others without allowing them to help us. But when others want to help us, we are threatened. Because our plan is at risk, we may react strongly to them.

Gentleness is the antidote to treat others with greater concern and to be less threatened by them.

Fear

We often equate gentleness with weakness. The King James Version translates *gentleness* as "meekness," and we inaccurately think *meek equals weak*. Some people appear to act with gentleness, while in truth they're afraid.

A patient at a dentist's office tried to lighten her fear by listing her middle name as "Wimp." A little later the receptionist stepped into the waiting room and said, "The doctor will now see the wimp." Four people got up.

We all face fear. Some freely admit it. Others run from the source of it. And some overcompensate by becoming angry, hostile, or loud. Many angry people operate under the assumption that no one will see through the mask of anger to their deep-down fear.

Christian gentleness isn't weakness; nor is it giving in to fear. Rather, gentleness uses God's strength to deal with our fear in the best manner, neither as a coward nor a bully.

Selfishness

The Greek word for gentleness is also translated "humility." When we believe we're greater and more important than others, our relationships suffer. When my friend and I discussed athletes we enjoy and those we don't respect, I noticed a common trait in the athletes I didn't care for: arrogance.

Gentleness in the form of humility gives us the ability to

have a balanced view of ourselves, to avoid the excess of conceit. Too much pride and self-absorption are roadblocks to deep relationships. Few want to spend much time with those whose main concern is self.

We all face these four natural tendencies. But we can counter them with God's own character trait of gentleness.

THE CHRISTIAN CHARACTER TRAIT OF GENTLENESS

Since there are so many differing and unbiblical views about gentleness, first we need to have a clear concept of how God defines it.

Gentleness Defined

Gentleness expresses itself in: "God-given strength to control our attitudes and actions, so we can deal with people according to their needs, not according to our own weakness."

Gentleness is a character trait that demonstrates a mild disposition and a temperate, considerate spirit. Gentleness chooses the best way to respond, without automatically becoming angry, harsh, or violent.

Gentleness is strength under control. Sometimes gentleness demonstrates itself with firmness and power, but that's a godly choice, not a natural reaction.

Gentleness includes humility, a refusal to place our desires above others.

Our society places a low value on gentleness as a character trait because people want power, strength, assertiveness. But God has a different perspective.

God Values Gentleness

Although we often view gentleness as weakness, God

141

doesn't. He considers gentleness to be a strength of great value and will reward us for it: "But *the meek will inherit the land* and enjoy great peace" (Psalm 37:11, emphasis mine). The meek end up with all the good stuff! Why? In part because they don't tend to kill themselves off, but more so because God cherishes meekness. We cannot be weak and accomplish inheriting the land.

Psalm 45:4 tells us God will act majestically on behalf of meekness: "And in thy majesty ride prosperously because of truth and *meekness* and righteousness; and thy right hand shall teach thee terrible things" (KJV, emphasis mine).

God also demonstrates how he rewards the humble: "For the Lord takes delight in his people; he *crowns the humble with salvation*" (Psalm 149:4, emphasis mine). Who gets saved? The humble. The gentle. The meek. Not the arrogant, the proud, the haughty, the violent and harsh people. The value of gentleness, upheld throughout the Bible especially with Moses and Jesus, has much to teach us today.

As Seen in Moses. Moses was more humble, or meek, than anyone else on earth (see Numbers 12:3). But he certainly wasn't weak. Raised in Pharaoh's court, Moses both possessed and used authority. Physically, he had enough strength to kill a man when defending a Hebrew slave. Emotionally, his anger flamed enough to do that.

Later in life, he consistently stood up to Pharaoh, who at that time was the most powerful man on earth. He had the personal power to lead over a million former slaves through forty years of wilderness wandering to the edge of the Promised Land. Even so, his anger sometimes got the best of him.

Was Moses a wimpy weakling? Not at all. He had power and strength, but in his later life it was clearly under the control of God. He didn't cave in to opposition, nor did he use his power selfishly against his opponents.

As Seen in Jesus. Remember who Jesus was. The Creator of the universe. The Son of God. Fully divine. At any moment, he could call down thousands of angels to carry out his wishes. Yet that power was under control. The prophecy about him in Isaiah 42:1-4 yields a picture of a gentle, quiet, humble person:

> Here is my servant, whom I uphold, my chosen one in whom I delight; I will put my Spirit on him and he will bring justice to the nations. He will not shout or cry out, or raise his voice in the streets. A bruised reed he will not break, and a smoldering wick he will not snuff out. In faithfulness he will bring forth justice; he will not falter or be discouraged till he establishes justice on earth.

Though he was the Creator, Jesus didn't have to be the center of attention, the life of the party. He wasn't loud and boisterous, although he did enjoy a good party. He treated the wounded with tenderness; people received comfort just by his presence. He was gentle with those whose spirit was a flickering spark that could easily be extinguished.

Even so, he was committed to justice, the hard edge of gentleness. His gentleness didn't cause him to ignore wrong and let it go on. He took a strong stand for righteousness out of a concern for all people. True gentleness doesn't cave in to evil but firmly uses the minimum power needed to enforce justice.

Both Moses and Jesus had power. Both could get angry. Yet they were in control, and they acted in gentleness — just as we should.

As Seen in Christians. God wants that same gentleness to begin in our new hearts and to spread outward until we consistently act gently. Although 1 Peter 3:3-4 refers to women, both sexes can possess a beauty that comes from a gentle spirit: "Your beauty should not come from outward adornment, such as braided hair and the wearing of gold jewelry and fine clothes. Instead, it should be that of *your inner self*, the *unfading beauty of a gentle and quiet spirit*, which is of great worth in God's sight" (emphasis mine).

Inner tranquility radiates into all we do, with gentleness as a central part of our character. But how do we actively cultivate the fruit of gentleness in our lives?

CULTIVATING AND NURTURING GENTLENESS

To become gentle, we first need to decide that since God values gentleness, we will as well. We'll never be gentle until it's our passion: "But you, man of God, flee from all this [selfish motivations], and *pursue* righteousness, godliness, faith, love, endurance and *gentleness*" (1 Timothy 6:11, emphasis mine). We cannot achieve gentleness until we flee selfish motivations.

Next, we must make gentleness a priority in the four areas of conflict, control, fear, and self-interest mentioned previously in this chapter.

In earlier chapters, we have examined the weeds that work against each godly character trait and then discussed specific steps we can take to nurture that trait. But for the fruit of gentleness, we'll modify the format. In each of the four areas, we'll deal all at once with what we need to weed out and ways in which we can nurture gentleness.

Conflict: Weeding Out Harshness, Nurturing Restraint

Because we all have rough surfaces of imperfection, we rub on each other and produce heat. Science calls such an action friction, and that is certainly what we have in interpersonal relationships. But incorporating gentleness into our character impacts how we handle conflict with others. Each of the following verses gives a slightly different angle on developing gentleness.

The message in 1 Corinthians 4:21 blends confrontation with sensitivity: "What do *you* prefer? Shall I come to you *with a whip*, or in love and *with a gentle spirit?*" (emphasis mine).

A gentle person refuses to use harsh means unnecessarily. But when needed, harshness doesn't contradict gentleness. Paul left the decision to the Corinthians regarding his gentleness or harshness. He would be as gentle as they would allow. But if gentleness didn't work, harshness would follow.

The key is not to start with harshness. Spanking children is a good example. Spanking has an effective and scriptural role in discipline. But to be most productive, spanking should be a last resort. We should begin with reasoning, time-outs, restrictions, and other appropriate measures. But if we start harsh, we can't get more intense without going over the line to abuse.

That principle extends to other relationships as well. We build gentleness into our character when, rather than first resorting to force, we become imaginative in discovering other ways to deal with conflict. Proverbs 15:1 tells us, "A gentle answer turns away wrath, but a harsh word stirs up anger." A gentle spirit will look for ways to express itself in conflict.

Gentleness certainly doesn't mean we ignore others' sins. It isn't the ostrich syndrome, where we don't want to know what's going on. Jesus dealt with justice in gentleness, and we can do the same: "Brothers, if someone is *caught in a sin*, you who are spiritual should *restore him gently*. But watch yourself, or you also may be tempted" (Galatians 6:1, emphasis mine).

Being gentle doesn't mean pretending evil doesn't exist. We deal with it with the most gentle and effective means. Our inner character of gentleness expresses itself. Many Christians today miss the injunction of 2 Timothy 2:23-25 (emphasis mine):

> Don't have anything to do with foolish and stupid arguments, because you know they produce quarrels. And the Lord's servant *must not quarrel;* instead, he must be kind to everyone, able to teach, not resentful. Those who oppose him he *must gently instruct,* in the hope that God will grant them repentance leading them to a knowledge of the truth.

A gentle person avoids quarrels. He may disagree, but he does so agreeably, with respect for the other. No matter what conflict we face, we never have a reason not to have an attitude of gentleness. When we don't allow people the freedom to disagree without being attacked, we change few minds. But when we gently and firmly express our beliefs and instruct people with respect, we transform conflict into something constructive. The key to dealing with conflict in a gentle way is to weed out harshness and to nurture restraint.

Control: Weeding Out Control, Nurturing God's Guidance

By nature, we want to be in control, and friction builds when others don't go along with our desires. A central tactic in building humility is weeding out our need to control. Gentleness grows when we give up being in charge and leave the control to God. Then we're not threatened by opposition (it's God's problem), and we can rest easy.

Psalm 25:9 says, "He *guides the humble* in what is right and teaches them his way" (emphasis mine). Who does God guide? Those who don't claim to know it all. Those who are open to God guiding their lives, rather than insisting on doing it on their own. The gentle are eager for God to lead.

But when we fight for our right to direct our lives, we lose gentleness. If we want to cultivate gentleness, we need to pull out the "I've got to look out for myself because no one else will!" weed. Otherwise we tend to see people as opponents when they don't advance our desires.

As we yield our desires to God and accept whatever he brings or allows into our lives, gentleness is able to grow within us. Because God is more knowledgeable and more wise than we are, his plans for us will always be better than our plans: "'For I know the plans I have for you,' declares the Lord, 'plans to prosper you and not to harm you, plans to give you hope and a future'" (Jeremiah 29:11).

When we truly believe those words, we won't see others as obstacles. We'll know God is in charge, for our best.

Fear: Weeding Out Fear, Nurturing Courage

Typically we respond to fear with either fight or flight, a heightened aggressiveness or a cowardly avoidance. Deep down, both are responses of weakness. True gentleness grows when we face difficulty, are aware of our fear, and stand up for what's right with the courage God provides. In doing that, we use only enough firmness or harshness to accomplish the God-given job. That's how Paul acted in 2 Corinthians 10:1-2: "By *the meekness and gentleness of Christ*, I appeal to you — I, Paul, who am 'timid' when face to face with you, but 'bold' when away! I beg you that when I come I may not have to be as bold as I expect to be toward some people who think that we live by the standards of this world" (emphasis mine).

Paul faced rebellion in Corinth that prompted fear in him. He didn't look forward to the encounter with eagerness. But Paul faced his feelings and told the people that fear wouldn't incapacitate him. He would be just as bold as necessary, despite his own tendency toward timidity.

Paul didn't run away, nor did he respond with heightened aggressiveness. Rather, God, the source of Paul's strength, gave him gentle courage to deal with the problem.

Gentleness grows into our character as we face fear, rather than running or overreacting. We learn we can stand up and use only the boldness needed, as Paul did.

Self: Weeding Out Selfishness, Nurturing Humility

We innately look at life from our own perspective, and that desire to get our way brings multiple difficulties to our relationships.

True gentleness translates into humility. We build that character trait as we take our inborn desire to advance ourselves, at the expense of others, and harness it with compassion for them: *"Be completely humble and gentle;* be patient, *bearing with one another in love"* (Ephesians 4:2, emphasis mine).

Humility ought not to be something we occasionally do, but something we consistently are. We're completely humble when we bear with others . . . when we consider their needs on a par with our own . . . when we're sensitive to their pain . . . when we express genuine concern in our conversations, rather than waiting to get our two cents in . . . when we accept their imperfections, just as we accept our own.

Babies begin with total self-absorption, thinking the world revolves around them. Maturity moves us toward balancing our needs with others'. Gentleness grows into a character trait as we humbly value others as we value ourselves and regularly act on that value.

Gentleness isn't easy, nor is it valued by the world. But God wants us to be as gentle as he is—not just to do gentle things, but to be gentle people. Not wimps, not cowards. Not bullies, not selfish. Just people who face adversity with godly courage and control.

After a tiring flight, a woman had a long layover at London's Heathrow Airport before the next leg of her journey. Buying a cup of coffee, a package of cookies, and the morning paper, she sat down at a table to enjoy all three. Soon she heard a rustling noise. Looking over her paper, she saw a young man helping himself to her cookies. She didn't want to make a scene, but neither did she want to lose all her cookies.

She leaned over and took a cookie. More rustling from the other side of the paper indicated he had taken another, too. Before long, just one cookie was left. Calmly he broke it in two, pushed half toward her, ate his, and walked away.

She was still quietly fuming when her flight was called. Upon gathering up her stuff, she found . . . her bag of cookies. She had been eating his!

Of the two, which one acted in gentleness and humility? Each of us needs to do the same for the people whose lives we touch.

Steps Toward Character Change

1. Have you ever felt like fighting? Describe the situation and your response. Do you think you were justified in making that response?

2. What did "being gentle" mean to Moses? to Jesus? What does it mean to you?

3. On a scale of 1 to 5, with 1 representing "I have no gentleness" and 5 representing "I most often respond with gentleness," how would you score yourself? Why?

4. In which of these four areas do you struggle the most to be gentle? Give an example.
   - conflict
   - control
   - fear
   - selfishness

5. How much do you value gentleness as a character trait?

6. What weeds most threaten to choke out gentleness in your life? How can you begin to pull those weeds?

7. How does God's kind of gentleness relate to
   - selfishness
   - courage
   - meekness
   - restraint

   In what ways can allowing God to guide your life build more gentleness into your character?

8. Talk with someone you trust about an area of your life in which you need to be more gentle. Brainstorm about specific ways to build gentleness into that situation or relationship—then act on those plans in the coming week.

CHAPTER 11

Doing What
We Most Desire

Self-Control

But the fruit of the Spirit is . . . self-control.
— PAUL THE APOSTLE, in GALATIANS 5:23

The face and name of a onetime date I had when I was single has faded with the years. Where we met is equally unknown. But one memory remains fresh. I had said I wanted to do something but wasn't able to.

She replied, "My big brother [her world revolved around her big brother and his marvelous wisdom] says we all do what we want."

I disagreed, somewhat strongly as I recall. Perhaps I possessed some jealousy toward this unknown wise man, or maybe it was just my tendency to take the opposite side for the sake of discussion.

But after our discussion, I recognized truth in what she said. We look at our options, weigh the benefits against the price we pay, and then do what we most want.

A dental hygienist had a hard time removing nicotine stains from a patient's teeth. The patient explained she was trying to quit smoking, but she was having a difficult time. The hygienist revealed that she and her husband were trying to quit also and only allowed themselves to smoke outside the house.

"Does that help?" the patient asked.

"Yes, but we're getting tired of watching TV through the patio doors."

We do what we want. The pleasures of smoking exceed the desires for health and comfort. Smokers know the danger, but the current pleasure is more important than the possibility of future cancer.

In areas of my life, I also tend to do what I want. Each morning I try to get to the gym by 7:00 A.M. I've learned that a forty-seven-year-old needs it. But often I struggle, and I confess I'm not fully successful. I hate to leave my bed, especially when leaving it will bring bodily pain and discomfort. But I'll eagerly get up at 3:00 A.M. for a fishing trip. Why? Fishing is fun, relaxing, and not painful like working out. Fishing is worth getting up for. I'm not so sure working out is. We do what we want.

One of the greatest dangers to our society, and particularly to the church of God, is a lack of self-control for the "good things." The growing debt spiral demonstrates we want what we want when we want it. We find it difficult to say no to ourselves. We struggle even to say "later." A commercial for an agency that clears credit records proclaims, "You deserve the American good life." What is that elusive "American good life"? The freedom to never have to say no to yourself.

Few people, including Christians, control their sexual desires until marriage. Even in marriage, we don't always say no to our desires (one study revealed that 31 percent of married people commit adultery). Violence increases at an alarming rate.

God offers an alternative: to implant his own trait of self-control, through the Holy Spirit, into our character. But controlling ourselves isn't easy.

OUR NATURAL TENDENCY:
TO DO WHAT'S EASIEST

As humans, we often tend to go with whatever is easiest. While in the Sierra Nevada Mountains, my dad and I often fished the Owens River, a slow stream meandering through cow pastures and sagebrush. During our drive there a local radio station broadcast this quote: "Following the path of least resistance tends to make men, women, and rivers crooked."

The crookedness of the Owens demonstrated that truth. And a lack of self-control reveals the same truth about people. The need for self-control impacts two areas: doing harmful things and doing good things excessively.

Doing Harmful Things

All temptations to sin promise fun, pleasure, and some benefit. Without those promises, we wouldn't do harmful things so often. But if we don't control ourselves, the long-term price exceeds the benefits because we violate God's moral law. God prohibits us from doing harmful things to protect us, since each sin also carries the seed of our own destruction.

Sex outside marriage leads to a breakdown of the family as the key building block for society. Adultery destroys the trust necessary for true intimacy. Lying eliminates the honesty required for people to work together. With these acts, we need to use self-control at all times because they clearly are wrong. Unfortunately, the frequency with which we do them is equally clear. Acts considered sinful twenty-five years ago are now held up as praiseworthy, or merely as an alternative lifestyle.

All around us we can see examples of people who don't exert self-control.

Doing Good Things Excessively

When properly used, many things are necessary for life, bring godly pleasure, and are good. But if we don't practice self-control in the "good things," too, they can become deadly issues of sin. When out of balance, even good things can control our lives. That's the message Paul gave to the Philippian believers: "For, as I have often told you before and now say again even with tears, many live as enemies of the cross of Christ. Their destiny is destruction, *their god is their stomach*, and their glory is in their shame. Their mind is on earthly things" (Philippians 3:18-19, emphasis mine).

Notice the semi-hidden warning in the middle of these verses. When we allow ourselves to use good things excessively, like our appetite for food, even good things can become our god. They can become the main desire of our lives, possessing us. Our god can become our stomach . . . or our sexual organs . . . or our bed.

We need food, but when done to excess it's gluttony. The proper use of sex is a tremendous joy and blessing, but outside marriage it's immorality. We need rest and leisure, but too much is laziness. We need money to live, but we can slip over the line into greed.

Almost any good thing can be abused. Although these things aren't morally wrong, the problem arises when we don't exert self-control. Since the problem arises from within us, the solution also rises from within. It is only as we value and practice godly self-control that we can become who God designed us to be.

THE CHRISTIAN CHARACTER TRAIT OF SELF-CONTROL

The apostle Paul frequently used sports examples in describing the Christian life, and the athletic imagery he used in 1 Corinthians 9:24-27 to describe the need for self-control is no exception:

> Do you not know that in a race all the runners run, but only one gets the prize? Run in such a way as to get the prize. Everyone who competes in the games goes into strict training [self-control]. They do it to get a crown that will not last; but we do it [self-control] to get a crown that will last forever. Therefore I do not run like a man running aimlessly; I do not fight like a man beating the air. No, I beat my body and make it my slave [self-control] so that after I have preached to others, I myself will not be disqualified for the prize. (emphasis mine)

Although the word *self-control* isn't found in these verses, the concept certainly is. In those verses we find the two primary components of godly self-control: our desire for God's best, and acting on that desire. We'll use what we discover to distill a definition for godly self-control.

DESIRING GOD'S BEST: A COMPELLING GOAL

All run in the race of life, but only a few run with passion. We begin to cultivate the character trait of self-control when we have a goal important enough that we must use self-control to arrange our lives to reach that goal. That's what Paul meant when he said, "Run in such a way as to get the prize" (1 Corinthians 9:24). In other words, pay the price. The goal is worth it.

The Olympic Games demonstrate that vividly. Teenagers give up a normal social life to practice hours a day, on top of their schooling. Some even leave their families to live and train with the best coach, hoping they'll be the one person out of hundreds to win the gold.

We develop the character of God when we embrace a goal that captures our lives, like passionately getting to know God. All we do should flow from that ambition. Remember, we do what we want.

We ought to want righteousness enough to resist sexual temptation; a healthy body enough to resist overeating and no exercise; Bible knowledge enough to commit time to study; our friends to come to Christ enough to risk their disapproval.

The principle of embracing goals applies to each aspect of the Christian life. If we don't fight temptation or eat right or study or share Christ, those things aren't that important to us. But what power can keep us from doing them? God provides the power if we want to use it. We must remember what Paul said in Philippians 4:13: "I can do everything through him who gives me strength."

Paul exhorts us not to jog in the race of life, not to amble along. Instead, we should grab life by the throat, seize the day, grab all the gusto we can, go for the gold. We should choose a goal for life so great that we need to control our lives to get it. Athletes do that for a temporary prize (see 1 Corinthians 9:25). But their valued laurel leaf withers after their moment of glory.

However, if we're willing to go for godly gold, the prize available to us is a victorious life now and in heaven later.

CONSISTENT EFFORTS:
ACTING ON OUR GOAL

Halfhearted efforts to reach all God intends for us won't

achieve our goal. Just like receiving an Olympic gold medal requires great effort, so does receiving God's awesome prize—not in the sense that we work to earn the prize, but that we work in cooperation with him.

Isn't that what Paul said in 1 Corinthians 9:27 about conquering his body through self-control so he wouldn't be disqualified for the prize? Spiritual diligence, struggle, and self-control are vital.

Again, athletes do that. They go into strict training, diet, exercise, and practice. They build their lives around reaching their goal. They eliminate anything that might keep them from it. And their goal doesn't begin to match ours. Achieving God's best for our lives requires the same difficult and consistent efforts athletes give. Being lackadaisical won't make it: "And without faith it is impossible to please God, because anyone *who comes to him* must believe that he exists and that he rewards those who *earnestly seek* him" (Hebrews 11:6, emphasis mine).

How do we find God's best for us? By seeking God with earnestness. By shaping our lives to best reach our goal, to do what we most want to do. Paul didn't aimlessly run in place; he ran for the finish line. He didn't shadowbox; he went for the knockout. He wanted to use all his energy to accomplish something: the prize of knowing God.

To do that, he beat his body and made it his slave. That doesn't mean he physically abused his body, but that he said no to its desires. He didn't let physical desires drive his life. Through discipline and self-control, he took charge of his body to accomplish what he most wanted.

I'm sure part of him wanted to sleep in. As a single man, part of him probably wanted to take advantage of the free sex Corinth was famous for. Part of him assuredly said, *Paul, use your learning and intellect to build a secure retirement.*

157

But Paul consistently made the efforts needed to train himself in self-control and godliness. Not merely as a wish, but as something he acted on. As someone once said, "If wishes were horses, then beggars would ride." Wishes alone get us nowhere. If we want to ride, we need to add will to our wish.

If we desire self-control, we need a compelling goal to build our lives around. And we need consistent efforts to reach that goal.

SELF-CONTROL DEFINED

So what is self-control? Self-control is choosing a godly goal for our lives, and doing whatever it takes to reach it. An anonymous author wrote:

> Self-control is what transforms a promise into reality. It is the words that speak boldly of your intentions. And the actions which speak louder than words. It is making the time when there is none. Coming through time after time, year after year. Self-control is the stuff character is made of; the power to change the face of things. It is the daily triumph of integrity over skepticism.

Godly self-control wants God above all, coupled with a willingness to do what he requires to gain his best. This control isn't based on our own willpower and determination. Rather, the trait of self-control comes from our decision to value God and to use his power to make our changes.

God won't do it for us until we make the first step. Self-control means stepping off wherever God says step, even when we can't see what's next. But self-control chooses to do whatever God tells us, even when it seems impossible, it doesn't make sense, or it's the opposite of what we would prefer to do.

Self-control desires the best, even when it's difficult and we would rather take it easy. Self-control requires continuing, when we would rather quit. Self-control puts God first, when we would rather reign on the throne.

For most of us, self-control doesn't come easily. So God helps us to cultivate it in our character.

CULTIVATING SELF-CONTROL

Paul describes the people in Philippians 3:18 as those who serve themselves and their natural appetites. Without self-control, they can't seek God or experience his abundance. Two paragraphs before, in verses 12-14, he contrasts those who live with self-control:

> Not that I have already obtained all this, or have already been made perfect, but *I press on* to take hold of that for which Christ Jesus took hold of me. Brothers, I do not consider myself yet to have taken hold of it. *But one thing I do:* Forgetting what is behind and *straining toward* what is ahead, *I press on* toward the goal *to win the prize* for which God has called me heavenward in Christ Jesus. (emphasis mine)

Notice the order Paul gave. First, he recognized that, although he wanted to be, he wasn't there yet. To get there, he had to give up some things, including forgetting anything in the past that would be an obstacle. Second, he pressed toward the goal. He worked hard at what was most important. He had a consuming passion to reach the prize.

Paul was cultivating self-control, and he put all his energy into his efforts. He carefully crafted his life to be most effective. If we desire to develop self-control in our lives, we need to do the same.

Weeding Out Saying Yes to Self
Self-control will grow only when we learn to say no to ourselves. Many of our desires work against God's best for us. Are we willing to give them up to build a greater passion for God? If we truly want to be who God designed us to be, we must say no to self.

Not only does cultivating self-control mean that we'll need to say no to self; it also means we'll need to say yes to some difficult things, such as spending more time with our families instead of climbing the corporate ladder at work.

NURTURING THE FRUIT OF SELF-CONTROL
Paul did a masterful job at "forgetting what is behind" in order to "press on toward the goal to win the prize." But he didn't just eliminate weeds; he added a goal. To nurture self-control, we also need to establish a purpose in life, a purpose with enough passion to guide all we do.

We Need to Choose Our Goal
Many life goals alluringly beckon us, encouraging us to take life easy; be comfortable; be financially secure; make it to the top of our profession; meet our physical desires; be respected and admired by others.

But for Christians, our life goal comes with our name, *Christ*ian. In Philippians 3, Paul revealed that his life goal was to be in heaven with Jesus. He ruthlessly eliminated anything that would work against that, courageously added anything that would help it, and sacrificially controlled his body and desires.

Valuing God so highly gave Paul the motivation for self-control. Wanting God more than anything else gives us the power to do the same. When Jesus was asked what was most important in a godly life, he responded by describing the normal Christian life: "Love the Lord your God with *all your heart and with all your soul and with all your mind.* This is the first and greatest commandment" (Matthew 22:37-38, emphasis mine).

We call that passion because it drives all we do. In the kingdom of God, we don't have to be intelligent, talented, or gifted. The best ability is availability to God with a passion to be used however he desires. We must be willing to do whatever it takes, whatever the difficulty, whatever the sacrifice.

Every day we face character decisions. *Which act is most moral? Which best expresses godly self-control?* Those decisions need to be evaluated by the question *Which of these will bring me closer to my life goal and which will pull me away from it?* On that basis we can make our decision and choose our action.

We Need to "Just Say Yes"

Once we've decided to say no to self, once we've established a life goal, then we need to say yes to whatever helps us achieve that. Self-control involves acting on whatever moves us closer to our godly goal. Remember the athletes in 1 Corinthians? They had a goal, and they did all they could to reach it.

But sometimes self-control means we also need to say yes to things that may decrease our leisure time, our financial security, our comfort. For each of us, the mix will be different. We begin as individuals with varying functions and ministries, different talents and energy levels.

As a result, exactly how we say yes will vary. But the process is the same. We build self-control deep down into our character as we decide that knowing and growing in God is more important to us than anything else in life. Then we continue to craft our lives to express that.

We say no to anything that hinders our goal. We say yes to anything that advances it. And we continue that pattern until the tendency becomes a trait of our character.

Bob Moorehead of the Overlake Christian Church in Washington wrote a powerful description of a person with self-control:

> I am a part of the "Fellowship of the Unashamed." I have Holy Spirit power. I've stepped over the line. The decision has been made. I am a disciple of his. I won't look back, let up, slow up, back away, or be still. My past is over, my present is busy, my future is now. I am finished with low living, sight walking, small planning, smooth knees, colorless dreams, tame visions, mundane talking, chintzy giving, and dwarfed goals.
>
> I no longer need preeminence, prosperity, position, promotions, plaudits, or popularity. I now live by presence, learn by faith, love by patience, lift by prayer, and labor by power.
>
> My face is set, my gait is fast, my goal is heaven, my road is narrow, my way is rough, my companions few, my mission clear. I cannot be bought, compromised, detoured, lured away, turned back, or delayed. I will not flinch in the face of sacrifice, hesitate in the presence of adversity, ponder at the pool of popularity, or meander in the maze of mediocrity.

I won't give up, shut up, let up, or slow up until I've preached up, prayed up, paid up, stored up, and stayed up for the cause of Christ. I am a disciple of Jesus. I must go till he comes, give till I drop, preach till all know, and work till he stops.

And when he comes to get his own, he'll have no problem recognizing me.

How much do you want a life like this? It's your choice. Decide now to partner with God in growing the trait of self-control.

STEPS TOWARD CHARACTER CHANGE

1. What is the driving passion of your life?
2. If it's true that we do what we most desire, what would others say is most important to you? Are you happy with that answer? Why or why not?
3. How would you define a "self-controlled" person?
4. In what physical area is it the hardest for you to exert self-control?
5. On a scale of 1 to 5, with 1 representing "I have no self-control" and 5 representing "I most often respond with self-control," where would you place yourself? Why?
6. What weeds most threaten to choke out self-control in your life? How can you begin to pull those weeds?
7. Do you struggle the most with doing wrong things or with doing good things excessively? Give an example.
8. What good thing could you accomplish if you said no to some harmful or excessive things in your life?

9. What do you think God most wants you to say yes to?
10. Ask someone you trust to help you develop a one-sentence passion statement that will give direction to your life. Then post that statement where you'll see it every day.

Making Character Changes

Grabbing God's Gusto

Being Filled with the Spirit

So I say, live by the Spirit.
—PAUL THE APOSTLE, in GALATIANS 5:16

My fingers formed an imaginary gun, pointed straight at my four-year-old grandson.

"Stick 'em up!" I said.

An eager smile spread across Joshua's face as his hands shot into the sky. He waited.

"Jump up two times" was the next command, and his year-old-sister, Hannah, giggled as her brother jumped to the sky.

"Now, hug your grandma and give her a kiss." Both grandmother and grandson enjoyed that one.

"Next, make a funny face at Hannah." The contortions of his face matched her grin of glee in seeing her older brother act so silly.

The game continued until all of us ran out of ideas, and we moved on to another activity. But I discovered something about Joshua that day. He quickly learned that "sticking 'em up" meant surrender, that you obey the person you raise your hands to.

That wasn't natural for Josh. The week before was the first time he told me to "Stick 'em up." I did, and he shot me! I had to explain how it worked, that raising your hands meant you give up in exchange for not being shot. You obey as a substitute for death.

With our games that day, Joshua demonstrated to me a secret about deep-down character change. Many of us raise our hands in worship. Whether we do it physically or symbolically, it serves as a sign of surrender to God in exchange for eternal life. But do we truly give up our lives to God? Only as we fully surrender can we receive the deep-down character change we've been talking about.

We've spent a lot of time looking at the need for us to work with God in changing who we are. We've examined the process of incorporating the nine character traits of God. One thing remains: to do what we've spent so much time talking about—to surrender fully to being the person God created us to be.

Have you ever wondered why some Christians just smolder? They attend, serve, and give, but they never seem to dig deep into God. They merely dabble at the surface of faith. Their faith is genuine, and they love God, but clearly something's missing.

Other Christians have a zest for God. Passion motivates their actions. In the midst of real difficulties, their smile reflects inner joy. They would never claim to be sinless, but sin is becoming less frequent. Deep-down character change is happening inside.

What's the difference? Why do some Christians have gusto in their faith and others don't? Why do some make the character changes we've talked about while others just stay the same? That's what we'll address in this final chapter.

OUR NATURAL TENDENCY: BORING CHRISTIANITY

To paraphrase Thoreau, any semiastute observer would see that most Christians "lead lives of quiet mediocrity."

For some people, Christianity is a duty—a good and necessary duty, but not something to get excited about. According to 1 Corinthians 3:1-3, many people allow themselves to be pulled in two directions:

> Brothers, I could not address you as spiritual but as worldly—mere infants in Christ. I gave you milk, not solid food, for you were not ready for it. Indeed, you are still not yet ready. You are still worldly. For since there is jealousy and quarreling among you, are you not worldly?

Paul addresses them as Christian "brothers," yet they were in two groups: spiritual Christians and worldly Christians. The worldly ones grabbed onto God with one hand—and the world with the other. They didn't fully surrender to God. As a result of their indecision, they missed out on the best Paul had to offer: solid food rather than the bland milk for spiritual babies. Because they weren't willing to let go of the world, they could make little progress toward closeness with God.

Bart, an intelligent and cautious fourth grader from the city, spent one summer visiting his country cousins. When they asked Bart if he wanted to ride their horse, Champ, Bart jumped at the chance.

Up close, the horse was much larger than the horses had seemed in the cowboy movies Bart had seen. Deciding to get onto the horse one small step at a time, Bart climbed on a rail fence in order to mount him. With one foot firmly planted on the fence, Bart threw his other foot over the saddle.

Champ didn't quite know what to make of this new way to be mounted. Slowly, he moved away from the fence, pulling part of Bart with him. Bart's caution kept him on the fence; his desire for adventure kept him on the horse — for a short time.

But his eight-year-old legs couldn't stretch forever. Soon he was deposited on the ground, right into a pile of manure. Why did he fall? He wasn't willing to surrender fully to the process of getting onto the horse.

The Christian life is the same. If we try to hold on to both the world and God, we fall into bad stuff.

Jesus vividly describes halfhearted Christians in Revelation 3:15-16: "I know your deeds, that you are neither cold nor hot. I wish you were either one or the other! So, because you are lukewarm—neither hot nor cold—I am about to spit you out of my mouth."

If you had talked with these church members in Laodicea, I'm sure they would have proclaimed both allegiance to and love of Christ. But to Christ, that wasn't enough. Jesus wants a fire in our soul, a fire that shows on the outside. He wants us to have a passion for being transformed into his character.

CHARACTER CHANGE: POWERED BY GUSTO

Achieving such a dramatic transformation of our character requires a strong motivation. Only an intense passion for

God can provide that desire to change. How do we build that gusto for God?

We can quickly summarize the process: Surrender to God produces passion. Passion then produces the motivation for deep-down character change. Spiritual gusto comes after we choose to be single-minded in our pursuit of God. Spiritual passion develops when we want God above all else, when we don't want to hold on to the world and God at the same time, when we're willing to go anywhere and be anything God desires, and when we want to incorporate God's character into ours.

The Bible calls that being led or filled by the Spirit. Only when the Spirit fills us can his fruit flourish in us. In our main text on the fruit of the Spirit, the apostle Paul gives a powerful description of the distinction between the Spirit-led life and the self-led life:

> Those who belong to Christ Jesus have crucified the sinful nature with *its passions and desires*. Since we live by the Spirit, let us keep in step with the Spirit. . . . So I say, *live by the Spirit*, and you will not gratify the desires of the sinful nature. For the sinful nature desires what is contrary to the Spirit, and the Spirit what is contrary to the sinful nature. *They are in conflict with each other,* so that you do not do what you want. (Galatians 5:24-25, 16-17, emphasis mine)

According to Paul, the solution to being torn in two directions is surrendering to God, allowing him to lead you in one direction, one step at a time. Notice also the warning: Either we gratify our sinful nature, or we gratify God's Holy Spirit. We can't do both, and our degree of passion for God comes from that choice.

171

In 1 John 1:8, we're given the tremendous promise that as Christians we will sin. Why is that promise tremendous? Because it frees us from perfectionism, the enslaving belief that we must be sinless to please God. True Christians still are drawn to the pleasures of sin, but they want God and his righteousness more. True Christians want to nurture the character of God within them more than they want to go on with "business as usual."

When we have this single-minded dedication to God, we build the passion and gusto that gives us the motivation to cooperate with the Holy Spirit in finishing the character changes he has begun in every nook and cranny of our lives.

BEING FILLED WITH THE SPIRIT

The experience of being filled with the Spirit started way back at Pentecost. On that day the sound of a violent wind was heard, tongues of fire touched the heads of the disciples, and they were filled with the Holy Spirit and spoke in other languages (Acts 2:1-4). This created such a stir that thousands rushed to check out the situation and were amazed at the exuberant joy and confidence shown by the Christians believers.

As we choose to walk with God and yield control to the Holy Spirit, we also can be filled with exuberant joy and confidence. We won't worry as much about pleasing people, and we'll be able to wear a smile — even in the worst of times. Once we've had a taste of the love, joy, and power the Spirit brings to our lives, why would anyone want to go back to a lukewarm walk with God?

As we're filled with the Spirit, we want more of God. We realize that in order to get more of God, he needs to get more of us. Walking with the Spirit through this lifelong process is how we grab God's gusto, how we build a passion to change our character deep down.

THE PROCESS OF BEING FILLED

We begin the process at our conversion, when we accept Jesus Christ as our Savior and Lord. At that point every Christian receives a life-changing gift: the Holy Spirit.

All Christians Receive the Spirit

Listen to the promise found in Acts 2:38: "Peter replied, 'Repent and be baptized, every one of you, in the name of Jesus Christ for the forgiveness of your sins. And you *will receive the gift of the Holy Spirit*'" (emphasis mine). At the time we give our lives to God, his Holy Spirit will come to live in us. He will provide power, teach, lead, comfort, and convict us of sin.

All Christians receive this tremendous gift. But not all Christians fully surrender, not all are on fire, not all get involved in deep-down character transformation. Some remain worldly believers, who are still infants (see 1 Corinthians 3). They have the Spirit, but they do not have the fruit of the Spirit. Why? Because they haven't completed the process. They've received the Spirit, but they haven't been filled with the Spirit. To make these deep-down changes, we need to surrender fully to the Spirit.

All Christians Can Be Filled, but Not All Are

In Ephesians 5:18 Paul commands Christians to go deeper in the Spirit: "Be filled with the Spirit." Paul would have no need to command something that happens automatically to all Christians, so by his statement we know that not all Christians are filled with the Spirit. Rather, being filled is a choice for each Christian.

Being Filled with the Spirit Is Not a Charismatic Gift

Being filled with the Spirit doesn't mean speaking in tongues or expressing what is popularly known as the charismatic gifts. Verses in 1 Corinthians 12:28-31 clearly indicate that not all Christians speak in tongues, not all are apostles, prophets, or miracle workers. But all Christians *are* to be filled with the Spirit. So we're talking about two different experiences. Being filled is for all Christians; charismatic gifts are not.

Being Filled Is a Continuing, Voluntary Surrender to God

What does it mean to be filled with the Spirit? The Greek grammar used in Ephesians 5:18 indicates that being filled is not something we do once for all, where one filling completes the job. Rather, being filled with the Spirit is an act that must be repeated to receive the maximum benefit.

When we yield our lives to the Holy Spirit, we recommit ourselves daily to put God first in our lives and to be the person God wants us to be. We also allow the Holy Spirit access to any hidden rooms in our hearts.

Just last week my wife, Sheila, and I had some friends over for dinner. The house was neat, clean, dusted, freshly vacuumed—and the study doors were firmly shut. Not one of our guests could have guessed that walking into the study meant taking their lives into their hands. We had shoved the loose ends of several unfinished projects in there, hoping no one would look!

Sometimes our spiritual lives are like that. Inviting Jesus into our lives is somewhat like inviting him into our house. At first glance, everything looks pretty good; we've cleaned all the main rooms. However, we have a secret junk room where we hide thoughts and acts we don't want him to see. We may even try to deny their existence to ourselves, locking our secrets behind a thick door. Being filled with the Spirit means we unlock those locks and open the doors—even when we're not quite ready to do so—because we want God's presence and character more than anything else.

CULTIVATING GUSTO

Being filled with the Spirit is essential to character change. But how do we do it? We become filled with the Spirit in three steps.

Ask Daily

To be filled with the Spirit, we merely have to ask, according to Jesus: "Which of you fathers, if your son asks for a fish, will give him a snake instead? Or if he asks for an egg, will give him a scorpion? If you then, though you are evil, know how to give good gifts to your children, how much more will your Father in heaven *give the Holy Spirit to those who ask him!*" (Luke 11:11-13, emphasis mine).

Filling us with the Holy Spirit is a request our heavenly Father is eager to grant. And we should ask him daily.

Jesus said, "If anyone would come after me, he must deny himself and take up his cross *daily* and follow me" (Luke 9:23, emphasis mine). Denying ourselves means to deny the preeminence of our worldly desires, deciding we want God more than anything else. Taking up our cross means we accept the course God establishes for us, including deep-down character change. Each day we need to give him permission to do whatever he knows is best for us and the kingdom.

Why must we do this daily? It's so easy to slide back into old patterns by semiconsciously taking back our lives from

God, one piece at a time. So, to be filled with the Spirit, each day we ask God to fill us, to lead us.

Repent from Sin

If we desire the Holy Spirit to fill us, we must remember he's called the *Holy* Spirit for a reason. We can't be filled with the Holy Spirit without a deep-seated desire to be holy. Holiness doesn't mean that we are sinless but that we pursue righteousness with passion and move away from sin, both in thought and deed.

A missionary worked with a tribe in Africa, and some became Christians. The tribal chief didn't accept Christ, but he closely watched how some people experienced transformation while others showed no change. He finally declared, "If being a Christian makes you a better person, you may remain so. If not, I forbid you to be a Christian at all!"

Without knowing the dynamics of the faith, that unbelieving chief had a clear idea of what true Christianity is all about: Character change accompanies genuine conversion.

Being filled with the Holy Spirit requires a heartfelt commitment to move away from sin and toward righteousness. One of the main roles of the Holy Spirit is to convict people of sin (John 16:8). How can we be filled with this Holy Spirit if we want to hold on to the sin in our lives at the same time?

In order to *receive* the Spirit, we need to repent, to turn away from sin (Acts 2:38). How much more must we turn away from sin if we want the Spirit to *fill us?* If we won't repent, it doesn't matter if we speak in tongues or raise the dead. We can't be filled with the Holy Spirit.

Gusto for God grows when we ask God daily to fill us with his Spirit and when we couple that with a genuine turning from sin.

Follow the Spirit

When we yield to the Holy Spirit, we don't resist what God wants to do in our lives. For instance, if we sing a song about raising our hands, we don't feel embarassed about doing it. We're not afraid to tell people we love Jesus. We don't hesitate to give or receive a holy hug. We joyfully give to someone in need. We respond to the problems in others' lives with sympathy and action. We develop a ministry in our church. To put it simply, we don't hold back from wherever God leads us through his Spirit.

That's the message found in 1 Thessalonians 5:19: "Do not put out the Spirit's fire." The King James Version tells us, "Quench not the Spirit." I particularly appreciate how J. B. Phillips translated that verse: "Never damp the fire of the Spirit." Clearly, the Holy Spirit wants to spark a fire in us. Our job is to be sure that we don't dampen that fire, that we burn with passion for God.

What does all this mean? It means that we don't fight against what the Holy Spirit wants to accomplish in our lives, including character transformation. It means that we don't look at the bottom line before we obey. It means that we don't search for reasons to say no. Rather, when God speaks to us, we look for reasons to say yes.

There's one caution: We must be sure it truly is God speaking to us! People attribute too many excesses to God when they should be attributing them to immaturity or to wanting to "hear" God say something we already desire. The Holy Spirit primarily leads from the book he wrote: the Bible. We need to study the Bible to ensure that where we believe the Spirit leads us squares with the Word of God.

Then, once we're sure it's the Spirit speaking to us, we can relax any inhibitions we have about following God and keep in step with the Spirit (Galatians 5:25). That's what it means to be filled with the Spirit. That's the source of gusto in our faith. And that is the key to our deep-down character change.

THE CHOICE IS UP TO YOU

Twenty-five years ago, I learned a lesson: Unless we open our lives fully to God, attempting to change our character will fail. But when we yield ourselves to God's Spirit, when we allow him to develop his fruit in our character, we'll experience spiritual ecstasy. We'll be the person God designed us to be.

Henry Varley said, "The world has yet to see what God will do with a man who is fully and wholly consecrated to Christ." If enough of us seek after deep-down character change, the world won't know what hit it!

Where are you in the deep-down character-change process? Have you surrendered to the Holy Spirit? Do you allow him to fill and lead you?

As you follow the Holy Spirit's leading, your passion for God will grow. You'll still have doubts and fears along the way, but God will walk with you. And he gives us the promise that we "can do everything through him who gives [us] strength" (Philippians 4:13).

With the Holy Spirit living within, providing power and filling us, we can accomplish all that God has in store for us. I challenge you to ask God right now to fill you with his Spirit on a daily basis, to commit your life to holiness, and to allow the Spirit to transform your character.

How about it? Will you begin the tremendous adventure to deep-down character change?